Reversing the Tide

Bold Moves in Climate Mitigation

By

Well-Being Publishing

WELL-BEING
PUBLISHING

To You,

Thank you

Table of Contents

Introduction: The Urgent Call for Climate Action

The mantle of responsibility to curb the adverse effects of climate change weighs heavily on all of our shoulders. The clarion call for immediate and robust action against this global menace can't be overstated. Within the pages of this pivotal discourse, we delve into the profound challenges that our planet faces and the monumental efforts required to tackle them.

Climate change represents one of the most pressing issues of our time, affecting every continent, ocean, and atmosphere layer. The consequences of a warming world are no longer distant possibilities but present realities that disrupt the lives, economies, and ecosystems across the globe. It's a multidimensional emergency, where melting ice caps and rising sea levels are as much a cause for concern as the sweltering heatwaves and devastating storms. The scientific consensus (IPCC, 2021) speaks to an uncomfortable truth: our planet's health is in precipitous decline, influenced in no small part by human activity.

Yet, amidst the sobering realities, this is no time for despair. This book serves as a rallying call, a blueprint for action that equips you, be you layperson or policy expert, with the knowledge and inspiration needed to make a tangible difference in this fight. We are, as it stands, at a crucial crossroads where the decisions and actions of today will indelibly shape the world of tomorrow.

Our society's past and current reliance on carbon-intensive energy sources has led to unprecedented levels of greenhouse gases in our planet's atmosphere, driving up temperatures and altering climatic patterns (Hansen et al., 2010). To secure a viable future, the need for a comprehensive and collective push towards carbon reduction can't be ignored. Whether through sweeping policy changes, innovations in science and technology, or far-reaching societal transformations, the tools for a healthier planet lie within our grasp.

But what does it mean to answer this urgent call for climate action? It starts with an informed citizenry ready to advocate for sensible policies and practices. Far beyond the bounds of personal efforts to reduce, reuse, and recycle, it encompasses a large-scale rethinking of how we interact with our environment. It's about the collective human spirit aligning behind a cause that transcends borders, beliefs, and backgrounds.

Climate action is about transforming the energy sector, harnessing the power of wind and solar, and revolutionizing transportation to lower emissions. It involves reshaping agriculture to both feed our growing population and heal the land. It demands an economic system that values sustainability and circularity over endless consumption and waste (Ellen MacArthur Foundation, 2013).

Perhaps most importantly, it necessitates an equitable approach. The effects of climate change do not impact all equally, with vulnerable and marginalized communities facing the brunt of environmental hazards. A just transition — one that provides new opportunities without leaving anyone behind — is imperative. It's about securing not just the environment but also social cohesion and economic viability for all.

Through the forthcoming chapters, this book will guide you through the complex landscapes of climate science and policy, international agreements, national strategies, and the myriad of innovations on the horizon promising a more sustainable future. It will showcase those who have already made strides in the right direction, offering case studies and lessons that can be replicated and expanded upon.

The succeeding chapters will not only present facts but also seed hope. You'll encounter stories of human ingenuity and resilience; tales of communities, cities, and countries that have embarked on the path to carbon neutrality. This book empowers you with a vision of what can be achieved when we channel our collective energies towards this shared goal.

Climate action is more than just a responsibility; it's an opportunity—an opportunity to forge a healthier, more equitable, and sustainable path forward for humanity. It's about envisioning a world where economic growth doesn't come at the cost of our natural environment, and where clean air and water aren't luxuries but guarantees.

As daunting as the challenge may seem, the momentum for change is building. From international accords to local grassroots movements, from the creation of green jobs to the financing of climate-resilient infrastructure, every arena of human endeavor has a role to play. This is a tapestry of transformation that we are all part of—weaving strands of action into a fabric strong enough to withstand the pressing weight of climate change.

To that end, each chapter dedicates itself to different facets of the climate crisis and the assorted mechanisms through which we can confront it. The journey through these pages is not simply an educational endeavor, but a catalyst for change. By closing the last page, you should not only understand the scales of the challenges ahead but also feel armed with the knowledge and inspiration to influence the trajectory of our shared future.

Let this introduction serve as the touchstone for what is to come. Recognize that while the onus to act may feel overwhelming at times, the collective power of motivated individuals and groups can, and has, tipped the scales in favor of progress and hope. Embrace this call — not merely with a sense of urgency — but with the conviction that every action, no matter how small, propels us closer to a sustainable future.

Now, more than ever, this urgent call for climate action is not just a whisper in the wind—it is a thunderous demand of our time—one that we must heed with courage, ingenuity, and an unwavering commitment to preserve and cherish our only home.

Chapter 1: Understanding Climate Change

As we heed the urgent call for climate action highlighted in the introduction, our journey begins with a crucial foundation—Understanding Climate Change. This chapter delves into the profound yet delicate tapestry of Earth's climate system, unveiling the truths of our warming world through a lens of irrefutable science. It is imperative to acknowledge that human contributions to greenhouse gas emissions are the potent accelerators of climate change, weaving a narrative of responsibility and opportunity (Smith et al., 2021). We peer into the essence of climatic shifts, dissecting how our industrial strides, energy usage, and deforestation practices tilt the balance of natural cycles. However, the power to rewrite our future is undeniably within our grasp. As we grasp the mechanisms of climate change and our role in them, we stand at the precipice of a critical paradigm shift—a shift that demands unwavering courage, innovative thinking, and collective action (Jones & Harris, 2020). This chapter does not merely aim to inform but to galvanize a movement, empowering each individual to channel knowledge into transformational change, for the path to redemption is paved with informed choices and strategic implementation. Let us embark on this essential quest armed with the insight necessary to forge alliances, inspire change, and ultimately steward the planet towards a sustainable equilibrium (Davies, 2018).

The Science of a Warming World

As we dive deeper into the fabric of our planet's climatic systems, it's imperative to understand the scientific underpinnings that map the contours of the current climate crisis. The Earth's climate has always experienced fluctuations; however, the rapid warming we now witness is unprecedented in the history of human civilization. Expanding our knowledge on this matter isn't just about being informed — it's about equipping ourselves with the power to catalyze change.

The average global temperature has increased by approximately 1.2 degrees Celsius since the pre-industrial era (Stocker et al., 2013). This change, though seemingly small, is a potent signal of the profound transformations occurring in our environment. The science is clear: greenhouse gases, such as carbon dioxide and methane, trap heat in the atmosphere, leading to a warming world (Stocker et al., 2013). Human activities, primarily the burning of fossil fuels and deforestation, have significantly escalated the concentration of these gases.

Complex climate models have been instrumental in dissecting the trajectory of future warming. These models are mathematical representations of the Earth's systems, tools that can point to the later chapters of our story if we continue on the current path. They predict not just hotter average temperatures, but also more extreme weather events, the loss of ice caps, rising sea levels, and shifts in biodiversity (Stocker et al., 2013).

The feedback mechanisms intrinsic to Earth's climate system can either dampen or amplify these changes. For example, melting ice reduces the albedo effect, lessening the planet's ability to reflect sunlight, which leads to further warming (Stocker et al., 2013). Such feedback loops are critical elements in our understanding, as they can potentially lead to tipping points, beyond which changes become irreversible.

One of the pressing issues associated with a warming world is ocean acidification. As the oceans absorb CO2, they become more acidic, which impedes the ability of marine creatures like coral and certain plankton to form shells (Stocker et al., 2013). These organisms are not simply individual casualties; they're foundational to the marine food web. When we disrupt the intricate balance of these ecosystems, we risk the wealth of biodiversity that sustains us.

To fathom the magnitude of the crisis, consider the arctic permafrost. Sequestered within this frozen ground is more than twice the amount of carbon currently suspended in the atmosphere (Schuur et al., 2015). Thawing permafrost has the potential to release colossal amounts of greenhouse gases, further fueling the cycle of warming. It's a stark reminder that the Earth's systems are deeply interconnected and that our actions reverberate through these links.

Heatwaves, droughts, and intense hurricanes are becoming the new normal. These phenomena are not merely points of data on a chart; they signify the loss of lives, homes, and livelihoods. The science tells us that if we stay this course, such extremes will only grow in frequency and ferocity (Field et al., 2014).

Yet, here's where our potential shines through. We have the capacity to understand these complex systems, predict their courses, and, most importantly, alter the trajectory. By advancing our use of renewable energy, innovating in carbon capture technologies, and reshaping our economies, we can steer towards a more sustainable future. But to enact these transformative changes, we must ground our decisions in robust scientific understanding.

Let's consider our atmosphere as a shared resource, a common thread running through humanity's collective journey. It's a source of life, protection, and connection, and we're tasked with the profound responsibility to safeguard it. When faced with the intricacies of climate models and predictions, it's easy to feel overwhelmed. Still, we must remember that in these numbers lie the answers to a more hopeful tomorrow — provided we act with conviction and purpose.

The journey toward mitigating climate change isn't linear. It's a complex interplay of science, technology, policy, and human behavior. As the stewards of this planet, we must embrace an unwavering commitment to learn, adapt, and implement. Each step taken is a step towards rebalancing our relationship with the world that sustains us.

Our understanding of this warming world is robust, but it's not just about the accumulation of knowledge; it's about the translation of knowledge into action. Empowerment grows from the fertile soil of understanding, and it is from this place that we can rise to meet the challenges that face us. It's time to accept the mantle of guardianship, to transform our concern into meaningful change, and to be the architects of a world that flourishes for generations to come.

Let this knowledge not culminate in paralysis, but in inspiration — a catalyst for innovation and a driving force for collaborative, global action. It's the commitment to this cause that will define the character and legacy of our time. We cannot afford to stand by as passive witnesses; we are the participants in writing the next chapter of our planet's history.

Understanding the science is the gateway to changing our world. In the coming sections, we will explore how human activities impact the climate, delve into international responses, and examine strategies for carbon reduction, all pivoting on the fulcrum of this scientific knowledge. With each step we take together, we shift the balance towards a sustainable future.

Human Activity and Its Impact on the Climate

The era that we're living in has been termed the Anthropocene, a period defined by human influence being the most dominant force shaping the environment and climate. The imprint of human activity is indelible, leading to an unprecedented change in the Earth's climate. In the span of just over a century, industrialization, deforestation, urbanization, and agriculture have jointly contributed to the amplified greenhouse effect that is the core driver of climate change (IPCC, 2021).

Our understanding of the atmosphere reveals that certain gases, such as carbon dioxide (CO_2), methane (CH_4), and nitrous oxide (N_2O), have the unique capacity to trap heat. Since the dawn of the Industrial Revolution, human reliance on fossil fuels for energy has caused concentrations of these gases to surge. Indeed, atmospheric samples show CO_2 concentrations have increased from about 280 parts per million in the pre-industrial era to over 410 parts per million today, levels that have not been seen for millions of years (Masson-Delmotte et al., 2021).

Modern transportation is another considerable contributor to greenhouse gas emissions. Vehicles powered by gasoline and diesel engines emit substantial amounts of CO_2 into the atmosphere. Aviation and shipping, while vital to our global economy, are also sources of significant emissions. Furthermore, urban sprawl has led to longer commutes and an increase in the number of vehicles on the road, further exacerbating the situation.

In the realms of industry and energy production, coal, oil, and natural gas have powered our economies but also unleashed vast amounts of CO_2. Electricity generation and heating systems based on fossil fuels are among the largest sources of global CO_2 emissions. The cement industry, indispensable for our urban development, chemically releases CO_2 as well and is responsible for around 8% of global emissions (Andrew, 2018).

Agriculture, while vital for feeding the planet, presents its own climate challenges. Land use changes, especially deforestation, make room for livestock and crops. In doing so, these activities not only release the carbon stored in trees but also reduce the planet's capacity to absorb CO_2 from the atmosphere. The cattle raised on these lands contribute to methane emissions, exacerbating greenhouse effects (Tubiello et al., 2021).

Industrial-scale production and the consumer economy have accelerated the emission of greenhouse gases still further. The extraction of raw materials, manufacturing, and waste disposal all release significant amounts of CO_2 and other chemicals into the atmosphere. Despite knowing these activities harm the climate, global production and consumption patterns continue at an ever-increasing pace.

The impact of these emissions is far-reaching. Climate change has manifested in more frequent and severe weather patterns, including hurricanes, heatwaves, droughts, and floods. The loss of polar ice and glaciers contributes to the rise of sea levels, threatening coastal communities worldwide. Ocean acidification, a result of CO_2 dissolving into the sea, imperils marine life and disrupts marine ecosystems.

For decades, scientists have warned that human activities are at the root of these changes. The Intergovernmental Panel on Climate Change (IPCC) has consistently identified human-made greenhouse gas emissions as the primary driver of climate warming (Masson-Delmotte et al., 2021). If left unchecked, the trajectory points to a future fraught with risk for all forms of life on Earth, including human societies and economies.

Acknowledging the gravity of our influence on the climate is pivotal. Yet, it is not just about awareness; it is about response. The choices made today, in energy production, transportation, agriculture, and consumer behavior, will either deepen the crisis or pave the way to a more sustainable and brighter future.

Inspirational figures and movements across the globe are already making headway. Renewable energy innovations are proving that the global economy can thrive without sacrificing the planet. Technological advancements in electric vehicles and solar and wind power are promising paths to a carbon-neutral future, ones that can inspire as much as they can revolutionize our world.

What is required now is an unwavering commitment to change, supported by policy, finance, and individual choices. Sustainability must be woven into the fabric of societies. Governments, businesses, and individuals alike must take responsibility and act decisively. This effort is monumental, undoubtedly, but the resolve of humanity has time and again proved equal to the task at hand when unity of purpose prevails.

Now is the moment to transform the legacy of the Anthropocene from one of disruption to one of restoration and rejuvenation. Embracing sustainable practices at all levels can ensure that human activity no longer spells disaster for the climate, but instead fosters an era of recovery and balance. Transformation is within our grasp; it's an ambition that calls for courage, innovation, and the best of human ingenuity.

This cause is not just imperative; it's exhilarating. To be poised at the cusp of such a critical exchange is not just a challenge; it is an opportunity—an opportunity to reimagine our world, an opportunity to redefine the parameters of progress, and an opportunity to ensure a livable planet for generations to come.

So let us embark on this path with determination, harnessing our collective strengths, and let every step reflect our commitment to this planet that we all call home. Together, we can mitigate human impact on the climate and steer towards a sustainable future — a future where we not only understand the profound effects of our actions but actively work to create a harmonious balance with the Earth's climatic system.

Chapter 2: The International Response to Climate Change

In the wake of a planet grappling with rising temperatures and calamitous weather patterns, the international community has risen to challenge the tide of climate change with a resilience and unity that befits the urgency of our times. The global response is a tapestry of agreements and protocols that bind nations to a common cause—the health of our Earth. Key climate pacts, such as the Kyoto Protocol and the landmark Paris Agreement, represent monumental leaps toward a cooperative and lasting solution to a global crisis. Within this framework, Nationally Determined Contributions (NDCs) serve as personalized roadmaps, tailored by each country, illustrating their commitment to reducing greenhouse gas emissions. The United Nations and its Intergovernmental Panel on Climate Change (IPCC) stand at the helm of these endeavors, offering scientifically backed guidance, rallying nations to a higher calling, and monitoring progress with an objective eye. As stewards of our shared home, the task before us is not merely one of policy and agreement, but an undertaking of transformative action that will carve a path to sustainability for generations to come (UNFCCC, 2015; IPCC, 2018).

Key Climate Agreements: From Kyoto to Paris

In the spirited pursuit of a sustainable future, the tale of international climate negotiations is marked by pivotal moments that have helped steer the course of our confrontations and reconciliations with the imminent climate crisis. The landmark **Kyoto Protocol**, adopted in 1997, served as the first significantly binding climate treaty, establishing legally enforceable targets for reducing greenhouse gas emissions for industrialized nations (United Nations Framework Convention on Climate Change, 1998). Yet, it was the **Paris Agreement** in 2015 that truly galvanized global commitment, as it encompassed both developed and developing nations in a unifying battle against rising temperatures, setting the ambitious goal to keep global warming well below 2 degrees Celsius (Rogelj et al., 2016). This transformation from Kyoto to Paris didn't just represent a shift in collaborative ambition; it reflected humanity's increasing acknowledgment of a shared destiny, where each nation's pledge through their Nationally Determined Contributions (NDCs) is a testament to the universal acknowledgment that the challenge of climate change can only be addressed by the indomitable spirit of collective global action and accountability (Falkner, 2016).

Nationally Determined Contributions (NDCs)

These are at the heart of the Paris Agreement, which represents a significant milestone in global efforts to address climate change. As we continue to unravel the international response to this pressing challenge, we must closely examine how these NDCs function as a dynamic tool for climate action.

Defined simply, NDCs are individual countries' commitments to reduce national emissions and adapt to the impacts of climate change. These pledges embody the efforts by each country to reach the overarching goals of the Paris Agreement—namely, to limit global warming to well below 2, preferably to 1.5 degrees Celsius, compared to preindustrial levels (United Nations Framework Convention on Climate Change, 2015).

What makes NDCs particularly powerful is their embodiment of progressiveness. Each country is expected to revisit and enhance these contributions every five years, infused with an ethos of collective ambition. The iterative nature of NDCs is not just about making improvements but is also a reflection of mutual learning and shared responsibility.

Indeed, the very essence of NDCs is rooted in self-determination, providing flexibility to countries in how they contribute to the global effort. Countries can draft their NDCs accounting for their national circumstances and capabilities. This intrinsic flexibility of NDCs encourages widespread participation, as it accommodates diverse economic and social contexts—recognizing the varied pathways countries may take towards a low-carbon future (Rogelj et al., 2016).

When delving into the actual content of NDCs, it's evident that they are not homogeneous—each NDC is as unique as the country that crafted it. This diversity can manifest in different mitigation strategies, from renewable energy adoption to deforestation prevention, each targeted to a country's specific profile and capabilities.

The success of NDCs is contingent upon transparency and accountability. Reporting on progress is not just about compliance; it's a commitment to international cooperation and trust. The ratcheting up process hinges upon countries' honest assessments and sharing of their experiences—trials, successes, and lessons learned (Falkner, 2016).

Influential to the integrity of NDCs is the complex interplay of domestic policy and international oversight. Aligning national policy frameworks with promises made on the international stage is an undertaking that requires formidable political will and forward-thinking leadership.

Critics might point out flaws and potential loopholes within the NDC framework—such as the lack of legally binding mechanisms to ensure compliance or the varying degrees of ambition among nations. These are real challenges that require continuous dialogue and enhanced cooperative mechanisms among parties.

However, it is imperative that we regard NDCs as instruments of hope and seeds of transformation. They are tangible expressions of each country's pledge to do their part, to engage in a collective battle against a global menace. These commitments can drive innovations, galvanize public support, and spark the domestic policy changes needed to achieve the broader objectives of the Paris Agreement.

Concrete action by industrialized nations in their NDCs sends a strong signal to their own industries and citizens, as well as the international community. When advanced economies lead by example, setting ambitious targets and deploying groundbreaking technologies, they not only pave the way but also assist others by lowering the costs of technologies and sharing best practices.

For developing nations, NDCs can be a gateway to sustainable development, combining climate action with economic and social agendas. The transformative potential for these countries is immense, as they can leapfrog to cleaner, more modern, and resilient economic structures. Effective climate action via NDCs, when coupled with financial and technical support, is an opportunity for these nations to avoid pathways of high-carbon development—aligning growth with global climate objectives.

Turning ambitions into reality requires robust financial mechanisms and investment. NDC implementation is an opportunity for governments, private sectors, and international institutions to collaborate—channeling funds, innovating financial instruments, and building capacity for those who need it most. Partnerships forged in finance are just as critical as those in technology transfer or capacity building (Buchner et al., 2021).

Furthermore, the peer pressure and internationally supported ambition cycles that NDCs induce can accelerate transformation. Countries observe each other's commitments and progress, motivating them not to lag behind. This dynamic is crucial in a world where, often, seeing is believing, and action begets action.

Let us not underestimate the power of these national pledges woven together into the international tapestry of climate action. NDCs present an inclusive framework for countries to define and design their paths to a sustainable and climate-resilient future—a future that's not dictated, but rather passionately authored by each nation, writing its own chapter in the story of our planet's salvation.

As we reflect on the profound nature of Nationally Determined Contributions, let's acknowledge the journey it ignites: one of constant improvement, shared responsibility, and renewed determination for every five-year cycle. The pledge of each country is a pledge to its citizens, to its future, and to the global community—a promise to pursue a world that's not just sustainable, but also equitable and thriving for all.

The Role of the United Nations and IPCC

The United Nations (UN) has been a cornerstone in the international response to climate change, serving as a global forum where nations can unite to address this critical issue. Its role extends beyond facilitation and into the implementation of significant policies and treaties aimed to mitigate the dangers of a warming planet. Anchored by key agencies within the UN framework, notably the United Nations Environment Programme (UNEP) and the United Nations Framework Convention on Climate Change (UNFCCC), these entities help to steer global climate policy and negotiations, fostering an atmosphere where every voice, from the smallest island nations to the largest economies, has a seat at the table (UNEP, 2021).

Essential to understanding the UN's impact is recognizing the gravitas the organization has in inciting collective action. The consensus-driven nature of the UN is its strength, empowering countries to adopt a unifying stance against climate change. This unity is crucial as we grasp for the fortitude to transform our societies in the face of this immense challenge. The UN's role in coordinating and galvanizing international efforts conveys a message of hope and possibility for a sustainable future (UNFCCC, 2021).

Within this context, the Intergovernmental Panel on Climate Change (IPCC) plays an indispensable role. Since its establishment in 1988 by the UNEP and the World Meteorological Organization (WMO), the IPCC has been the leading international body for the assessment of climate change science. Its assessments are landmark scientific endeavors, synthesizing thousands of peer-reviewed studies that detail the past, present, and future states of Earth's climate system (IPCC, 2021).

The reports provided by the IPCC serve as a compass for policymakers around the world, translating complex scientific data into actionable information. They are inherently motivational, not only cataloging the risks of inaction but also highlighting the myriad of solutions at our disposal. When we reflect on our mission to curb the progression of climate change, it is the findings of the IPCC that underpin our strategies and embolden our resolve (IPCC, 2021).

Through the UNFCCC, the UN has overseen the establishment of the landmark Kyoto Protocol and the seminal Paris Agreement. These frameworks reflect the international community's commitment to limit global warming and are pivotal in shaping the fight against climate change. They set out clear targets for greenhouse gas reductions, which translate into national policies and spur innovations in technology and sustainable practices (UNFCCC, 2021).

Part of the success of the UN and IPCC lies in their power to inspire. As nations come together, they create a fusion of solidarity and science, a blend that can fortify the will to undertake pivotal changes. They remind us that climate change is not just an environmental issue but a humanitarian one, affecting the food we eat, the air we breathe, and the economic systems that support our societies (UNFCCC, 2021).

The IPCC also plays an influential role in clarifying the consequences of climate inaction. By presenting an apolitical assessment of potential futures, it provides a scientific foundation upon which to build our understanding of climate risk. This knowledge acts as a catalyst for action, prompting deeper introspection and a call to mobilize across all sectors of society (IPCC, 2021).

The work of the UN and IPCC goes beyond conventional boundaries, permeating the realms of education, innovation, and cultural transformation. They are not simply arbiters of facts; they are harbingers of change, signaling the potential for a prosperous, sustainable future. Each report, resolution, and conference is a testament to their unwavering dedication to a cause that transcends generations and borders (UNEP, 2021).

Nationally Determined Contributions (NDCs) are a prime example of the influence exerted by the UN's climate-related machinations. Through the Paris Agreement, countries are expected to pledge, and progressively enhance, their strategies for reducing emissions and adapting to the impacts of climate change. It is through the meticulous orchestration of the UN that these NDCs are discussed, refined, and implemented, drawing a clear line between global policy and local action (UNFCCC, 2021).

However, the journey is far from over, and the UN and IPCC face ongoing challenges in mobilizing sufficient action to meet the targets set out in international agreements. The fight against climate change is fraught with complexity, and it requires unwavering commitment from all sectors. Persisting in this fight demands that we cling to the scientific roadmap provided by these bodies and translate their insights into tangible progress (IPCC, 2021).

The role of the UN and IPCC extends into encouraging transparency and accountability. Through mechanisms like the Enhanced Transparency Framework included in the Paris Agreement, they ensure that progress towards climate goals is measurable and verifiable. This creates a system where successes can be replicated and shortcomings addressed, vital for the iterative process of climate action (UNFCCC, 2021).

As we imagine the future, it's clear that the UN and IPCC will continue to be pivotal in orchestrating the symphony of efforts required to address climate change. They are tasked with the herculean effort of not only understanding and articulating the science but also in rallying the collective might of the global community (UNEP, 2021).

In conclusion, the role of the United Nations and IPCC in the international response to climate change cannot be overstated. Through their collective work, they've laid the foundation for global cooperation and provided the tools necessary for advancing climate action. The path forward is clear: we must continue to heed their findings and recommendations, remain steadfast in our commitments, and kindle the spirit of innovation and dedication that is needed to preserve our planet. Let the lessons we derive from their work guide our actions as we stride toward a brighter, more sustainable future for all (IPCC, 2021; UNFCCC, 2021).

Chapter 3: National Strategies for Carbon Reduction

As we pivot from the global orchestra of agreements and policies, Chapter 3 draws us into the vital realm of 'National Strategies for Carbon Reduction', where the indomitable human spirit meets the rigorous benchmarks of science. Within the confines of national borders, governments are architecting ambitious roadmaps designed to curb their carbon footprints, weaving sustainability into the fabric of economic, social, and political frameworks. Such national blueprints for a low-carbon future hinge on innovative policy-making, characterized by boldness and precision, to transform aspirations into measurable progress. They encapsulate targeted mitigation strategies, subsidies for green technology, and regulatory efforts to decarbonize key sectors, capitalizing on unique national circumstances to invigorate the march toward a resilient and sustainable future (Hsu et al., 2021). Yet, making headway requires surmounting intricate challenges: the harmony of economy and ecology, the equity of impact, and the coherence between short-term imperatives and long-term objectives. This chapter unlocks a treasury of empirically proven strategies that edify the significance of tailored approaches and resilient infrastructures in slashing down the gauntlet of emission curves (Rogelj et al., 2016). It's an inspirational compass for change-makers yearning to sculpt a world where economic vitality and carbon neutrality are not adversaries but allies in the quest for a thriving planet (Clark et al., 2018).

Setting and Achieving Ambitious Targets

In the trenchant challenge of climate mitigation, setting and achieving ambitious targets is not just wishful thinking—it is imperative for survival. Understanding the science of climate change and acknowledging the urgency is one thing; actualizing transformative policies is quite another. The transformative journey starts with setting robust, science-based targets that will steer nations toward a carbon-neutral future.

To set these targets, we need clarity of purpose. We must recognize the profound impact of human activities on climate change and understand that reversing these effects requires immediate and unswerving commitment from both the public and private sectors. The targets need to be SMART: Specific, Measurable, Achievable, Relevant, and Time-bound. These make the goals clear and actionable, enhancing the likelihood of achieving them.

Leaders across the world need to marshal expertise from various sectors to craft targets that resonate with both national priorities and global imperatives. For instance, the energy sector plays a critical role. By setting a target to move towards 100% renewable energy by a specific year, nations can align policies, investments, and innovation towards achieving this milestone (Smith & Lee, 2020).

However, setting a target is only the beginning. Achieving it calls for coherent strategies and robust action plans. Governments should spearhead these initiatives with decisive policies that create conducive environments for carbon reduction, such as subsidizing renewable energy, enforcing strict emissions regulations, and investing in research and development.

Transparent monitoring and reporting structures are vital to track progress towards these targets. The establishment of an independent body to oversee this process promotes accountability and ensures that all stakeholders are working cohesively toward the national goal. Ongoing assessment provides the opportunity to recalibrate targets and strategies when necessary.

It's not enough to appreciate the dire consequences of inaction. As a global community, we need to be ambitious in our attempts to shape a sustainable future. This means we also have to contribute to innovative funding mechanisms. The mobilization of finance in support of climate action cannot be overstated, whether it be through green bonds or the leveraging of private sector investments (Kumar et al., 2021).

Moreover, achieving ambitious targets is not the dominion of a single entity. It requires a concerted effort where governments, businesses, civil society, and individuals partake in a collaborative dialogue. Public-private partnerships can be particularly effective in deploying clean technologies and facilitating the transition to a low-carbon economy.

Education and public awareness should not be underestimated in the pursuit of these targets. Citizens empowered with knowledge and understanding are more likely to support and contribute to policies geared towards carbon reduction. It's critical that national strategies include comprehensive educational campaigns on energy conservation, waste reduction, and sustainable practices.

Ambitious targets also harness the innovation in transportation and energy sectors. Investing in electric vehicles, efficient public transit systems, and sustainable urban planning can significantly reduce carbon footprints while promoting health and quality of life for all citizens.

Countries should not act in isolation. International cooperation is a cornerstone of effective climate action. Learning from each other's successes and failures can help countries to implement the best practices in their carbon reduction strategies. This also involves enhancing capacities to develop local solutions to climate challenges.

Justice and equity are other important aspects of setting and achieving carbon reduction targets. Developed nations, having contributed more significantly to historical emissions, should shoulder a greater responsibility in assisting developing nations through technology transfer and financial support. Conversely, every country should ensure that its policies do not disproportionately affect the vulnerable sections of their population.

The pathway to achieving ambitious carbon reduction targets is fraught with challenges. However, the same ingenuity and persistence that powered human progress through centuries can guide us towards a sustainable future. We need to act with resolve and optimism, knowing that every step we take toward our objectives is a movement away from the brink of climate catastrophe.

Motivation, while crucial, needs to be backed by action. The world's future depends not only on the ambitiousness of our targets but on the sincerity and efficacy of our efforts to achieve them. National strategies that are flexible and adaptive, and yet robust and decisive, are critical in achieving the ambitious carbon reduction targets necessary to avert climate calamity (Brown, 2022).

We stand on the precipice of transformative change. With foresight, courage, and collective action, we can fulfill our moral and existential obligation to future generations. In the spirit of cooperation and with unyielding determination, let us all commit to setting and achieving ambitious targets for carbon reduction.

Case Studies: Success Stories and Lessons Learned

Within the quest to reduce our global carbon footprint, several nations have emerged as beacons of inspiration, piloting innovative approaches to slashing emissions and setting the pace for others to follow. These case studies serve not just as cheerleading stories but as concrete examples that the pathway to a low-carbon future is both viable and replete with opportunities.

Consider the success of Denmark, a pioneer in wind energy, which has transformed its energy system to rely heavily on renewables. Denmark set the ambitious target of being free from fossil fuels by 2050 and is well on its way, with more than 47% of its electricity consumption covered by wind power in 2019 (Jørgensen et al., 2020). This small nation's strategy was not just about installing turbines; it was about reshaping an entire energy culture focused on sustainability and community engagement.

Across the Pacific, we turn our gaze to Costa Rica, a country that has run on more than 98% renewable energy for consecutive years. With an aim to be carbon neutral by 2021, Costa Rica has shown a dedication to sustainability, initiating projects that protect biodiversity while engaging in reforestation efforts to offset emissions (Montero, 2018). Its National Decarbonization Plan outlines an economy-wide strategy, indicating that size is not a bar to ambition.

Further afield in the East, China's story tells a tale of scale and speed. Despite being the world's largest emitter of CO2, China is also the largest investor in renewable energy. In 2017, it announced plans to invest $360 billion in renewable energy by 2020, a move that not only cuts back on emissions but also propels the country to the forefront of the global clean energy market (Zhang et al., 2019).

Lessons can be drawn from Sweden, which has one of the lowest carbon footprints in Europe, thanks in part to its carbon tax implemented in 1991. This long-term and consistent pricing signal encouraged innovation and technological advancements, growing its economy while lowering carbon emissions (Andersson, 2019).

In the United States, the state of California demonstrates the power of subnational actors. Its cap-and-trade program, which puts a price on carbon emissions, shows how integrating economic incentives with environmental policy can lead to successful outcomes. As the world's fifth-largest economy, California's strides, including its goal to achieve carbon neutrality by 2045, broadcast a strong signal that economic prosperity does not have to come at the cost of the planet (Hanemann, 2020).

Norway's transportation transformation illustrates yet another facet of carbon reduction strategies. Through significant incentives, electric vehicles (EVs) accounted for 54.3% of all new car sales in 2020. This shift towards clean transportation, driven by government policy and consumer change, is part of Norway's broader goal to become carbon neutral by 2030 (Figenbaum, 2020).

Each of these success stories embodies a blend of audacity and pragmatism. They underscore that the course to carbon reduction is not just a technical endeavor but a collective journey grounded in policy innovation, international cooperation, and community-based action.

However, success is not without its setbacks and difficulties. For instance, the Danish wind energy miracle did not come without challenges in integrating renewable power into the national grid, requiring significant investment and technological development (Jørgensen et al., 2020). Likewise, while China's pivot toward renewables is commendable, its simultaneous expansion of coal power abroad paints a complicated picture of its climate leadership (Zhang et al., 2019).

Each case offers lessons in navigating the tension between progress and perfection. Costa Rica's delayed timeline for carbon neutrality—pushed beyond 2021—reflects the complexities inherent in translating vision into reality (Montero, 2018). Such moments remind us that strategies must be dynamic and adaptable.

Moreover, these cases demonstrate the importance of knowledge sharing and cross-border learning. As nations carve their unique paths towards decarbonization, it becomes evident that collaboration is inevitable and essential. Policies such as Sweden's carbon tax have inspired similar approaches in other countries, showing that leadership can be as contagious as it is influential (Andersson, 2019).

The journey to carbon reduction is an evolving narrative of trial and error, success and recalibration. It is a journey that requires us to boldly reimagine the architecture of our global economy and demands unwavering commitment to the principles of sustainability and equity. These stories are the touchstones in the unfolding chronicle of climate action, each page a testament to human innovation and resilience.

Importantly, these stories are not destined to remain exceptions. They are the forerunners to what could become the new normal—if we so choose. The lessons drawn from these narratives are powerful tools that can help tailor national strategies, shape international discourse, and spur collective action. Their most profound message is perhaps a simple yet daunting truth: what has been achieved can be emulated and surpassed.

The distillation of these lessons is crucial for policymakers, businesses, and individuals alike. They offer a roadmap to success, highlighting the need for clear, ambitious goals; inclusive planning that accounts for social impacts; strong and consistent policy signals; the importance of technological and financial innovation; and the transformative potential of community engagement and public participation.

As we reflect on these case studies, let us be inspired to act, to advocate, and to dare to lead the way in our communities. The stories of Denmark, Costa Rica, China, Sweden, California, and Norway are invitations to all who wish to heed the call for climate action. Let us take up the torch and write our chapters in the great global effort to safeguard our planet for generations to come.

As you step forth from this section to the next chapters, bear in mind that the success achieved by one nation can light the way for others. National strategies for carbon reduction can and should evolve from these shared success stories and lessons learned. The strategies work. The proof lies within the stories of countries that looked futureward and dared to dream of a cleaner, more sustainable world for all.

Chapter 4: Energy Transformation: The Shift to Renewables

In the heart of our struggle against climate change lies an undeniable truth: we must pivot from the carbon-emitting energy sources of yesterday to the renewables of tomorrow. The shift to renewables isn't simply a suggestion; it's a clarion call for survival, a transformation that signals hope for a cleaner, more resilient world (Jacobson et al., 2017). Imagine fields of solar panels and wind turbines not just dotting the landscape but defining it, harnessing the Sun's warmth and the wind's breath to empower our cities and industries. This chapter delves into that very transition, exploring how the empowerment of solar and wind energy as primary power sources is not only conceivable but increasingly inevitable. As we witness renewables outstrip coal and oil, becoming more cost-effective and efficient, we're not just participating in a market shift; we're nurturing the seeds of revolution in the very way we power our lives (IRENA, 2020). The energy transformation narrative isn't just technical; it's steeped in human ingenuity and bolstered by an unwavering resolve to champion a future that respects the delicate balance of our planet.

Solar and Wind: Powering the Future

As the vanguards of our renewable revolution, solar and wind power stand at the forefront, harnessing the boundless energy of the sun and the relentless force of air currents to fuel a brighter, cleaner tomorrow. These technologies epitomize resilience and innovation, charting a path towards energy independence and sustainability that aligns with our deepest values and our urgent need to address climate change. The advancement of photovoltaic cell efficiency (Lewis, 2021) and the proliferation of offshore wind farms (Kaldellis & Kapsali, 2020) signal a metamorphosis, transforming the way we power our lives while curbing the carbon emissions that imperil our planet. Visionary policies, strategic investments, and relentless pursuit of technological breakthroughs can propel us closer to a future where energy is plentiful, cost-effective, and in harmony with the earth's delicate balance, underscoring the imperative to shift gears now, and not a moment too late, before the damage becomes irreversible (Bogdanov et al., 2019).

Advances in Storage and Grid Technology

In our journey toward a sustainable future, the innovations in storage and grid technology play a crucial role as foundational pillars of the energy transformation. The shift towards renewables is a compelling narrative of progress, but it cannot take place without addressing the challenges that come with intermittent power sources like wind and solar. To make a real impact, these green giants must be supported by advanced energy storage solutions and a smart, resilient grid that can distribute electricity efficiently and reliably.

Energy storage systems are akin to the heartbeat of the renewables revolution. They allow us to capture energy when the sun is shining and the wind is blowing, and to use it when the demand arises—whether that is during peak hours or when the sky is cloudy, and the air is still (International Renewable Energy Agency, 2022). The advancements in battery technology, particularly lithium-ion batteries, have led to improvements in capacity, lifespan, and cost-effectiveness. Additionally, the exploration into alternative storage technologies like flow batteries, compressed air energy storage, and even the potential of hydrogen storage speaks to a future where energy storage is as common as the renewable sources themselves.

It's fitting to compare the smart grid to the circulatory system of this new energy age. A traditional grid operates in a relatively straightforward manner, with energy flowing from large power plants to consumers. However, a smart grid supports a two-way flow of electricity and data, enabling a more responsive and efficient energy distribution (U.S. Department of Energy, 2020). Smart grids can manage the variability of renewable energy production, reduce waste through better demand response, and even allow homes with solar panels to feed excess power back into the system.

Advances in grid technology, such as the development of microgrids, present solutions for energy resilience and security. Microgrids can operate independently from the central grid, which becomes particularly significant in the wake of extreme weather events—an increasing concern under climate change scenarios. The ability of these smaller grids to disconnect and operate autonomously protects communities against widespread outages and can be a bulwark of local sustainability.

Grid-scale energy storage is receiving unprecedented attention as a key enabler for decarbonizing the electricity sector. Lithium-ion batteries may be at the forefront, but other technologies like solid-state batteries and metal-air batteries are on the horizon. These have the potential to offer higher energy density and safety, lending even further credence to the pivotal role of storage in the future grid (Schmidt et al., 2017).

Digitalization of the energy sector is another transformative development in this narrative. Leveraging artificial intelligence and machine learning for predictive maintenance, optimized energy distribution, and advanced forecasting models will all be central to managing increasingly complex grids that integrate variable renewable energy sources (National Renewable Energy Laboratory, 2019).

Virtual power plants (VPP) signify a new epoch where disparate energy resources can act as a single power plant. By remotely and automatically dispatching and optimizing generation from various sources, they maximize efficiency and can quickly respond to changes in the supply-demand landscape. The growth of VPPs showcases the innovation and adaptability of grid technology in accommodating a renewable-centric world.

Another groundbreaking advancement is the concept of grid-interactive efficient buildings (GEBs). These buildings actively communicate with the grid to reduce, shift, or modulate their energy consumption in real-time. By doing so, they can alleviate stress on the grid during peak times and support the integration of renewables by acting as dynamic assets within the energy system.

Charging infrastructure for electric vehicles (EVs) is now becoming a vital component of grid services. Modern EVs can serve as mobile energy storage units that bolster grid resilience. Vehicle-to-grid (V2G) technology, where EVs can discharge electricity back into the grid, is not just a vision for the future but a reality being piloted in various regions. It holds the promise of turning EV fleets into a distributed storage resource that can help manage the variability of renewable energy sources.

When considering a world heavily reliant on renewables, energy equity and access become even more important issues. Grid advancements should not only aim for technological prowess but must also ensure that energy is accessible and affordable for all—a critical step toward a just and equitable energy transition that leaves no one behind.

Interconnectivity between regional grids is also expanding the potential of renewable energy. By linking grids over larger geographical areas, energy can be redistributed from surplus to deficit regions, effectively mitigating the imbalance between energy production and consumption. This leads to a more resilient overall system that can handle the fluctuations inherent in renewable energy sources.

The potential for offshore wind farms to contribute vast amounts of clean energy is awe-inspiring, but only feasible with the development of sophisticated, high-voltage direct current (HVDC) transmission technology. HVDC enables the efficient transfer of electricity over long distances with minimal losses, connecting remote renewable energy harvesting sites to major population centers (Qiu et al., 2021).

Finally, the concept of energy as a service rather than a commodity is manifesting through innovations in grid technology. Companies are beginning to offer energy reliability and management services, thereby shifting the focus from mere energy sales to providing an integrated service that assures efficiency, stability, and sustainability of the power supply.

With each leap forward in storage and grid technology, we are crafting the building blocks for a sustainable future—one where clean, renewable energy is the norm, and where electricity is not just a utility but a driver of equitable growth and environmental stewardship. These technological advances, underpinned by scientific ingenuity and an unwavering commitment to the planet, illuminate the path to achieving the global ambitions of carbon reduction and climate resilience. They leave us not just hopeful but charged with the energy to make a difference, to advocate for policies, and to implement strategies that will lead us into a greener, more secure tomorrow.

The Decline of Fossil Fuels and the Role of Divestment

The transition towards sustainable energy sources is not only a matter of innovation but also a concerted movement away from the infrastructure that has long supported fossil fuels. This chapter delves deep into the inevitable decline of fossil fuels and explores how the divestment movement is accelerating this descent, changing the financial landscape, and empowering the surge of renewable technologies.

Over the years, humanity has come to realize that our reliance on fossil fuels is unsustainable. The burning of coal, oil, and natural gas for energy contributes massively to greenhouse gas emissions, with catastrophic consequences for climate and ecosystems (Ritchie & Roser, 2020). With an increasing global temperature, the need for a drastic reduction in carbon emissions has never been clearer, propelling the rise of renewable energy sources such as wind and solar.

Renewables are now not merely an alternative, but they're increasingly seen as the best choice. The economics of energy production are witnessing a tectonic shift – solar and wind power are now on par with or cheaper than fossil fuels in many parts of the world. The competitive cost of renewables, paired with the understanding of their environmental benefits, is driving an energy revolution (Lazard, 2020).

But there's another silent force at work here, one that speaks directly to the financial institutions and investors worldwide: divestment. Divestment is the opposite of investment – it means getting rid of stocks, bonds, or investment funds that are unethical or morally ambiguous. When it comes to fossil fuels, divestment is a powerful statement that an investment firm or individual investor can make to show that they do not support the harmful impacts of these industries.

It's not just a symbolic gesture, but a strategic financial decision. Fossil fuel companies are facing a 'carbon bubble'. As the world moves towards a low-carbon economy, assets tied up in fossil fuels are at risk of losing their value. Divestment helps protect investors from this financial risk (McGlade & Ekins, 2015).

Moreover, divestment sends a loud signal to companies and policymakers. When institutions such as universities, religious organizations, or pension funds divest, they add to the societal pressure on fossil fuel industries to change their business models or become obsolete (Ansar et al., 2013). This sort of activism by investment strategies indicates a clear shift in societal values – a declaration that financial returns cannot come at the expense of the planet's future.

The impact of divestment movement has been profound. By the end of 2020, over 1,200 institutions across the globe representing more than $14 trillion in assets committed to divesting from fossil fuels (Fossil Free, 2020). This growing wave of commitments is tightening the financial tap for fossil fuel companies, making it harder for them to raise capital for new fossil projects.

This financial shift is accompanied by increasing regulatory pressure. Governments around the world are introducing policies to reduce greenhouse gas emissions, such as carbon pricing, which directly affects the profitability of fossil fuel projects. As these regulations become more stringent, the economic advantages of renewables become even more pronounced. The divestment movement has likely influenced these policy directions, highlighting not only the ethical but also the economic rationale for leaving fossil fuels in the ground.

The role of divestment is critical in the transformation of our energy systems. As fossil fuel investments become less attractive, capital is redirected towards clean energy technologies. This influx of investment spurs innovation in renewables, driving down costs and increasing deployment. It's a self-reinforcing cycle – the more we divest from fossil fuels, the more feasible and profitable renewable energy becomes.

Undoubtedly, this transition presents challenges, especially for communities and workers directly tied to the fossil fuel industry. This is where just transition strategies come into play, ensuring support and retraining for workers, as well as economic diversification for communities that have historically relied on fossil fuels (Heffron & McCauley, 2018). Divestment should be seen as part of a wider strategy that includes support for those most affected by the energy shift.

The decline of fossil fuels is also a story of resilience and opportunity. It opens up doors for new industries, for innovation in energy storage and efficiency, and for the creation of millions of jobs worldwide in renewable sectors. The trajectory is clear, but the pace must quicken. Divestment is one of the levers that activists, investors, and concerned citizens can pull to accelerate the move toward a cleaner and more equitable energy future.

Let's be clear: time is not on our side. We've witnessed extreme weather events, loss of biodiversity, and dire scientific warnings that tell us we're on a dangerous path. But we can change course. Divestment isn't just about withholding money from fossil fuel companies – it's about investing in the future of our planet, in the air we breathe, the water we drink, and the ecosystems that sustain us. Herein lies the motivational force—each dollar diverted from fossil fuels is a step towards the world we aspire to create.

It's about seeing the future not as a distant, abstract image, but as the very real outcome of the decisions we make today. The decline of fossil fuels should be perceived not with fear of the unknown, but with a compelling optimism about the possibilities inherent in the transition to renewable energy. This transition, bolstered by thoughtful divestment strategies, is key to our aspirations for a sustainable planet.

As we close this chapter on energy transformation, remember—we're not waiting for some hero to save us. We're the architects of our future, and divestment is one of the many tools in our arsenal. When combined with bold leadership, technological innovation, and broad public support, divestment can help dismantle the old carbon-intensive infrastructure and pave the way for a sustainable, just, and healthy world.

Chapter 5: Innovation in Transportation

Advances in transportation technology serve as powerful levers for climate action, transforming hope into tangible strides toward sustainability. Momentum is building behind electric vehicles (EVs), which promise not only to curb emissions but also to redefine mobility as we know it (Sperling & Gordon, 2009). Yet the innovation path isn't limited to electrification; groundbreaking developments in materials science, energy efficiency, and integrated transport systems are rewriting the agenda for future cities and reshaping societal norms (Jacobson et al., 2021). Embracing these transportation innovations isn't just an option—it's an imperative for all of us committed to carving out a future where blue skies are no longer a rarity, but the norm. As we delve into the specifics, remember that every forward-thinking plan has the potential to become a pivotal chapter in our collective journey towards a more resilient and vibrant planet.

Electric Vehicles: Steering Towards a Cleaner Future

As the symphony of innovation in transportation crescendos, electric vehicles (EVs) eloquently exemplify humanity's capacity to harmonize technology with environmental stewardship. Embracing electric vehicles isn't merely an adoption of a new mode of transit; it's a profound shift towards a future unshackled from the restraints of fossil fuel dependency—a future where the air is cleaner, cities are quieter, and carbon footprints shrink with every silent mile driven.

The surge in electric vehicle interest isn't serendipitous; it's the result of conscious choices by innovators, policymakers, and a society that's increasingly aware of climate change's perils. Battery electric vehicles (BEVs) and plug-in hybrid electric vehicles (PHEVs), which run on electricity entirely or partly, stand as beacons of hope in a world grappling with the urgent need to decarbonize(Sperling & Gordon, 2009). The shift to electric vehicles is essential not only in lowering greenhouse gas emissions but also in catalyzing a broader cultural and economic transformation.

Think of the internal combustion engine—a symbol of the 20th-century industrial achievement—as a paragon awaiting retirement. With each passing year, electric vehicles reap the benefits of incremental scientific advancements, growing economies of scale, and enhanced consumer awareness. These factors collectively lower costs and improve the electric vehicle's accessibility and attractiveness to the mainstream market(Bloomberg New Energy Finance, 2019).

Transportation electrification isn't aspirational; it's transformational, boasting the capacity to revolutionize the way we interact with our environment. A paradigm shift remains at our fingertips, with electric vehicles promising a significant reduction in air pollution, a problem doggedly persistent in urban centers worldwide. Electric motors are inherently more efficient than their combustion-engine counterparts, meaning that EVs can significantly reduce energy use and emissions—even when factoring in the electricity production mix(McKinsey & Company, 2020).

Moreover, it's not simply about swapping out gas tanks for batteries. Electric vehicles can play an integral role in the envisioned smart grids of the future, where they can act as mobile energy storage units. This interactivity enables them to contribute to grid stabilization and the integration of intermittent renewable energy sources such as solar and wind power(Kempton et al., 2008).

While the environmental benefits are crystal clear, the impetus for EV adoption also includes energy security. By reducing dependency on imported oil, countries can buffer themselves from volatile global markets and geopolitical strife. Localized energy creation from renewable sources, paired with electric vehicles, offers a robust strategy for a more secure, reliable energy future with a significantly diminished risk profile.

Autonomy in transport also translates to economic revitalization. A robust electric vehicle industry can stimulate job growth in new and emerging sectors ranging from automotive manufacturing to energy services. It can rekindle a spirit of innovation reminiscent of the space race, but this time, the finish line is a sustainable planet (International Renewable Energy Agency, 2017).

The EV transition, however, isn't without its challenges. Achieving widespread adoption involves surmounting economic, technical, and behavioral hurdles. Upfront costs, though decreasing, still pose a barrier. And the development of a ubiquitous charging infrastructure is critical in allaying range anxiety—the fear of running out of power mid-journey. Building this infrastructure requires significant investment and coordination between public and private stakeholders.

Another salient factor is the source of electricity. To maximize electric vehicles' environmental and health benefits, the electricity that powers them must come from renewable and low-carbon sources. This necessitates a concurrent escalation in renewable energy production and distribution capacities, aligning the timeline of EV adoption with the clean energy transition.

It's worth noting that the production of EV batteries does have an environmental footprint, chiefly in the mining of rare metals such as lithium and cobalt. Addressing these concerns calls for ethical sourcing practices, investments in battery recycling technologies, and continued research into alternative materials and methods that tread more lightly on our planet's finite resources.

Regardless of these hurdles, projections show a steep growth curve for EVs in the coming decades. The projection isn't baseless optimism but grounded in current trends and policy commitments by nations striving to meet climate goals. Electric vehicles are rapidly moving from niche to normal, fueled by an unprecedented alignment of technological capability, market dynamics, and policy-driven demand (International Energy Agency, 2020).

Consumer awareness and preference will act as the rudder that guides this ship forward. As social narratives around EVs shift from a luxury novelty to a practical and moral imperative, individual choices will accumulate into collective transformation. It's a story of empowered consumers taking the wheel, quite literally, and driving the market towards sustainable solutions.

The ultimate benefit of this push toward electric vehicles extends beyond the tangible. It's about inspiring a belief that innovation, harnessed thoughtfully, can lead society to a confluence of ecological balance and technological progress. In the race to decarbonize transportation, electric vehicles aren't just participants; they are, decidedly, the frontrunners steering us towards a cleaner, brighter, and more sustainable future.

Indeed, the road ahead is long and winding, but electric vehicles light the path forward—a path that beckons with the promise of clear skies over thriving cities, of economies that flourish without damage to the earth that sustains them. Let us embrace this wave of change with the courage and vision it deserves, for it is in our power to engineer the future we aspire to—a future where the hum of an engine no longer drowns out the voices of the world pleading for change.

Public Transit and Urban Planning Solutions

The march towards a sustainable future is undeniably interconnected with the transformation of our transportation systems and the re-envisioning of urban planning. Within the labyrinth of climate action strategies, establishing robust public transit and adopting forward-thinking urban planning are pivotal. Public transit not only offers a reduction in individual carbon footprints but also encourages a cultural shift toward collective responsibility. Meanwhile, urban planning and design aim to create environmentally friendly, economically vibrant, and socially equitable cities.

The synergy between public transit and urban planning has been proven time and again as a climate change combatant. A well-designed public transit system can significantly decrease the number of personal vehicles on the road, leading to lower greenhouse gas emissions (Schäfer et al., 2019). However, an effective transit system extends beyond mere availability; it includes considerations of accessibility, reliability, and affordability which are key determinants of public adoption.

Urban planning plays a complementary role to public transit. It's not merely about having buses and trains crisscrossing a city but also about the urban environment that they operate within. A city planned with public transit at its core promotes denser, more walkable neighborhoods. High-density living reduces the demand for sprawling suburban developments, often a source for increased vehicular emissions due to longer commutes and the loss of carbon-absorbing green spaces (Newman, 2020).

Moreover, the urban landscape must be envisioned as a tapestry of green infrastructure. This includes the integration of parks and green roofs, which not only sequester carbon but also provide a cooling effect, further mitigating urban heat islands typically exacerbated by excessive concrete landscapes. The benefits are multifold, enhancing the quality of life while aligning with climate goals (Foster et al., 2011).

For example, cities like Copenhagen and Amsterdam are renowned for their bike-friendly streets and robust public transportation networks. When the infrastructure supports safe and convenient non-motorized transportation, citizens are more inclined to opt for bikes over cars for daily commuting. Such cities stand as testaments to the transformational power of conscientious urban planning and the embrace of greener transit options.

Tackling the innovation in public transportation also means looking at multimodal transit solutions. Effective urban planning creates seamless links between different modes of transport. A commute may start on a bicycle, connect to a train, and finish on a bus, with minimal wait times and a user-friendly interface to coordinate it all. This kind of integrated system can dramatically enhance the appeal of public transportation (McCormick et al., 2013).

While delving into the fabric of urban environments, it's crucial to consider the social implications of transit and urban policy. Equity must be a guiding principle, ensuring that public transportation serves all segments of the population, particularly those in lower-income communities often underserved by current transit systems. Urban planning has the power to not only reduce emissions but also to build greater community cohesion and inclusivity by giving all residents access to the same high-quality transit options (Litman, 2020).

Advancements in technology also promise to revolutionize public transportation. Electrified public transit can lead to zero-emissions buses and trains. When paired with renewable energy sources, this could render public transportation networks carbon-neutral. Furthermore, innovations in smart city technologies can optimize route planning and reduce wait times, enhancing efficiency and public engagement with transit systems (Santos et al., 2010).

Transitioning toward sustainable transportation and urban development requires a cultural evolution as well. Citizens must adopt a new mindset where shared mobility is seen as a collective step towards a healthier planet. Public awareness campaigns, education, and community programs can help foster this shift in perspective, empowering individuals to make choices that benefit the community and the environment.

Financial incentives can be a powerful lever for change, encouraging public transportation use and smart urban development. Subsidies for transit, zoning incentives for mixed-use developments, and penalties for high-emission vehicles are all potential policy tools. These fiscal strategies must be carefully crafted to avoid unintended consequences, focusing on long-term sustainability over short-term gains.

Urban planners and policy-makers face the daunting task of retrofitting and adapting existing infrastructure. The challenge is twofold: to introduce new, green features into cities and to ensure that current infrastructure is not only maintained but also aligned with new sustainability standards. This often requires significant investment, as well as thoughtful reimagining of legacy systems to meet modern needs without exacerbating existing inequalities.

The journey towards integrating public transit and urban planning in the fight against climate change is complex and multifaceted. It requires stakeholder engagement at every level, from government agencies to private developers, from community organizations to individual citizens. Collaboration is key, leveraging the diverse perspectives and expertise of all involved to craft solutions that are as innovative as they are effective.

In summary, the metamorphosis of our urban habitats into sustainable ecosystems is a tremendous opportunity. Through concerted efforts in public transit enhancements and urban planning revolutions, we can reimagine our cities. We have the capacity to create spaces that breathe life into sustainable practices, make room for nature within our concrete realms, and give rise to communities rooted in equality and environmental stewardship.

The realization of sustainable transportation and urban development is not only a matter of technological innovation but also a reflection of our commitment to future generations. As we chart a path towards a climate-smart world, let public transit and urban planning be the twin beacons that guide our way. Let these solutions resonate with the legacy we aspire to leave—a world not just survived, but thrived in, harmoniously and holistically with all its inhabitants.

Chapter 6: Building a Sustainable Economy

The vast canvas of our economic structures, long marred by an unsustainable exploitation of resources, is now being repainted with the vibrant hues of sustainability and resilience. In this crucial chapter, we dont just dream of an economy that values the environment – we blueprint an actionable plan. The ascent to a sustainable economy demands the embrace of a circular economy model, a transformative approach where waste is repurposed and resources are managed sustainably; such a model stands as a pillar of hope against the relentless tide of climate degradation (Geissdoerfer et al., 2017). By leveraging technological advances and economic incentives, we fuel the creation of coveted green jobs, igniting a powerful engine for growth that harmonizes with our planet's rhythms (Jackson, 2017). Yet, the journey doesn't end with job creation; it marks the beginning of a persistent quest for innovation, inspiring industries and individuals alike to redecorate the economic landscape with the vibrant, lasting colors of sustainability. This chapter therefore serves not as an elegy for what was, but as a resolute declaration of what must be: an economy that thrives within Earth's ecological limits and empowers every stakeholder to sow the seeds of a future that's fertile with possibility (Raworth, 2017).

The Circular Economy Model

Envision the thriving economy of the future: one where every product is designed for multiple life cycles, resources are regenerated naturally, and sustainability is positioned at the core of every business decision.

The Circular Economy Model paints this vibrant picture, offering a transformative approach to production and consumption that stands in stark contrast to the traditional linear 'take-make-dispose' methodology (Webster, 2015). In this model, materials constantly flow in closed loops, energy is renewable, and innovation is persistent (Geissdoerfer et al., 2017). Change-makers, this is where you cue your leadership; by embracing circular principles, businesses can pivot towards strategies that not only curb emissions but also unleash new opportunities and value chains. It's about harnessing the power of restoration and regeneration, where waste becomes an archaic concept and resources are utilized with reverence and foresight. The circular model breaks the bounds of what was once thought possible, revealing that the goal isn't merely to mitigate damage, but to create economies that thrive in harmony with the Earth's cycles, ensuring longevity and prosperity for both the planet and its inhabitants (Stahel, 2016).

Waste Reduction and Sustainable Resource Management

As we dive into the heart of building a sustainable economy, it's crucial to focus on two intertwined facets: waste reduction and sustainable resource management. In this modern era, the preservation of our environment and the prudent usage of resources are not just options but imperatives for survival. The strategic reduction of waste and sustainable management of resources act like two sides of the same coin; fostering a circular economy where materials are reused and regenerated, emulating the natural cycles of our planet (MacArthur Foundation, 2017).

Incorporating sustainable resource management starts with the fundamental understanding that resources are finite. The extraction and processing of raw materials impact the environment significantly through habitat destruction, pollution, and by contributing to carbon emissions (Schandl et al., 2018). Therefore, curtailing the need to extract by reducing waste and consumption is a direct line to climate change mitigation.

One of the pivotal components in reducing waste is preventing its creation. A preventive approach directs us to mindfully design products that are durable, repairable, and upgradable. The moment we shift our perspective to view waste as a design flaw, we begin to innovate solutions that substantially decrease the waste stream going into landfills and reduce the greenhouse gas emissions associated with waste decomposition.

An excellent example of waste reduction is the implementation of extended producer responsibility (EPR) programs. EPR policies require manufacturers to be accountable for the entire life cycle of the product, including the end-of-life phase. This responsibility encourages companies to design products with easier recycling in mind or take on the recycling process themselves, thus reducing waste significantly (Lindhqvist, 2000).

Sustainable resource management also advocates for the maximization of product life cycles. Every product has a lifecycle which, if extended, can help reduce overall waste production. Encouraging a culture of repair, refurbishing, and repurposing not only saves the consumer money but also prevents resources from becoming waste prematurely. The growing popularity of repair cafes and community tool-lending libraries exemplifies how community action can contribute to these goals.

Reducing food waste is another critical area that demands attention. Roughly a third of food produced worldwide is wasted (FAO, 2019), and when wasted food decomposes in landfills, it generates methane, a greenhouse gas far more potent than carbon dioxide. Solutions such as improved food storage technology, efficient distribution systems, and consumer education about food use and preservation play a high-stakes role in reducing the carbon footprint of our food systems.

When waste cannot be eliminated, we turn our sights to recycling and composting. Effective recycling programs keep materials in circulation, reduce the demand for new raw materials, and lower greenhouse gas emissions. Composting organic waste converts it into a valuable resource for soil amendment, improving soil health and helping sequester carbon.

At a larger scale, the industrial sector must also transition toward more sustainable practices. Industrial symbiosis, where the waste of one company becomes the feedstock for another, demonstrates the creative potential for sustainable resource management. This system turns what was once considered waste into a valuable input, minimizing environmental impact and fostering a zero-waste economy (Chertow, 2000).

Water, a vital yet scarce resource, requires vigilant conservation methods. Innovative water-saving technologies and effective water management strategies such as rainwater harvesting, wastewater reuse, and precision agriculture can dramatically reduce water consumption and enhance community resilience against droughts and water scarcity.

Energy resources also need to be managed sustainably. Energy conservation and efficiency measures, along with the transition to renewable energy sources presented in earlier sections, underscore the symbiotic relationship between energy policies and waste reduction strategies. Efficient energy use leads to less demand for energy-intensive materials and thus less overall waste.

As these approaches are implemented at various scales by individuals, businesses, and governments alike, it's vital to ensure broad access to information on sustainable practices and to incentivize behavior that aligns with resource management objectives. Economic incentives, such as tax breaks for businesses that operate sustainably, can drive market-based solutions to resource management challenges.

The role of education in changing consumption patterns cannot be overemphasized. Education enables consumers to make informed decisions, choose sustainable products, and adopt lifestyles that prioritize the economy of use over the economy of abundance. Awareness campaigns and educational programs redefine what consumers deem important, leveraging social norms and values for the betterment of the environment.

In conclusion, as we advance into uncertain times with climate change, we can't underestimate the power and potential of waste reduction and sustainable resource management. These practices serve not only to protect the natural world but as testimonials of ingenuity and humanity's capacity to adapt and thrive sustainably on this Earth. The actions we take today in managing our resources will echo into the future and define the health and prosperity of our planet and generations to come.

Green Jobs and Economic Incentives for Sustainability

Imagine a world where each and every job contributes to healing the planet, restoring ecosystems, and building resilient communities. It's not a distant dream; it's a necessity. And this necessity is birthing an era of green jobs—a cornerstone of the sustainable economy we're collectively striving to build.

Green jobs stand at the intersection of economic progress and environmental responsibility. They're jobs that not only provide workers with decent wages and safe working conditions but also significantly reduce environmental impacts (International Labour Organization, 2018). They're present across all sectors, from renewable energy to sustainable agriculture, and they hold the promise of a better future for all.

These jobs are part of a burgeoning industry, fueled by innovation and the unwavering spirit to correct our course towards a more sustainable future. But how do we ensure that the growth of green jobs is not just an addition but a transformation of the economy? The answer lies in creating robust economic incentives for sustainability.

By prioritizing policies such as carbon pricing, subsidies for renewable energy, and investment in green infrastructure, governments can stimulate demand for green jobs. These incentives not only encourage businesses to adopt environmentally friendly practices but also drive entrepreneurial activity in the clean tech space (IRENA, 2020).

The workforce must be ready as well. Reskilling and upskilling programs are crucial. As the demand for jobs in renewables, energy efficiency, and other sustainable industries grows, so too must the availability of training and education opportunities that empower workers to transition from sunset industries to sunrise ones.

Incentives also come in the form of tax credits and deductions for companies that adhere to sustainability standards. This can supercharge businesses to not just meet regulatory requirements but exceed them, embedding sustainability into the core of their strategies and operations.

Furthermore, special economic zones focused on sustainability can attract businesses and capital, functioning like incubators for innovation and hubs for the green economy. These zones offer a concentrated space where policies and incentives can be optimized and where new ideas can bloom.

It's also essential that we design these incentives with fairness in mind. A just transition ensures that no community is left behind in the switch to a renewable and sustainable economy. This means supporting historically disadvantaged or fossil fuel-dependent regions with tailored approaches to sustainable development, from community-based renewable energy projects to education and retraining initiatives.

The journey doesn't stop with domestic policy, either. International collaboration can amplify the impact of incentives. When nations align sustainability standards and coordinate investment strategies, they can create a ripple effect that accelerates the global expansion of the green economy (Klein et al., 2018).

Impact investing is another sphere where economic incentives meet sustainability. Private capital can provide the funds necessary to scale green technologies and business models at pace with the urgency of the climate crisis. By offering competitive returns for investments in sustainability-focused ventures, the financial market can mobilize vast amounts of capital to where it is most needed.

There's also an essential role for consumer behavior. Demand for sustainable products and services fuels green jobs. When we choose to buy products with a lower carbon footprint or services that prioritize eco-friendliness, we're essentially voting with our dollars for a greener economy.

Let's not forget the social dimension of green jobs. They offer opportunities for more inclusive economic growth, engaging underrepresented groups and providing them with avenues to contribute to and benefit from the sustainable economy. By integrating equal opportunities into sustainability incentives, the green transformation becomes a powerful tool for social equity.

What's ahead is a vision warmly embraced by millions, where economic growth and job creation are inextricably tied to environmental and social stewardship. This vision requires deliberate action, collaborative effort, and forward-thinking policies—an economic structure reinvented for sustainability.

To transform this vision into reality, policies and practices must evolve continuously. We can't be content with simply planting the seeds of sustainability; we must nurture them into a flourishing canopy of green jobs that support livelihoods and protect our planet.

In essence, green jobs and economic incentives will be the sunlight and water for the sustainable economy's growth. Through these mechanisms, we are fabricating a world that aligns with the values of responsibility, resilience, and renewal—a world where every job is a step towards a sustainable future for generations to come.

Chapter 7: Agricultural Practices and Food Security

In the pursuit of food security amid a changing climate, Chapter 7 explores the transformative potential of sustainable agricultural practices. We delve into the essence of regenerative agriculture, a holistic approach that rebuilds and revitalizes the soil, sequestering carbon and enhancing biodiversity (Lal, 2020). Through this practice, not only can we significantly mitigate the effects of climate change, but we also bolster our resilience against its impacts. We must reimagine our relationship with the land, moving away from extractive methods that deplete, towards nurturing practices that restore. As we embark on this journey, we explore the symbiotic relationship between diet and sustainability, understanding how a global shift towards plant-based diets can dramatically reduce methane emissions and alleviate strain on our planet's resources (Clark & Tilman, 2017). Through the integration of cutting-edge science and the rekindling of ancestral wisdom in harmony with the Earth's rhythms, we can forge a future where agriculture is a wellspring of sustainability and a bastion against climate adversity. The call is clear: we must bravely transform our agricultural systems to feed humanity and heal the planet in equal measure.

Regenerative Agriculture and Carbon Sequestration

We now turn to a concept that holds the potential to transform the heart of agriculture and its relationship with the planet: Regenerative Agriculture and Carbon Sequestration. This transformative approach goes beyond mere sustainability; it is an embodiment of the art and science of encouraging the land to heal itself, fostering ecosystems where crops and nature coexist in beneficial symbiosis.

Regenerative agriculture refers to farming and grazing practices that, among other benefits, reverse climate change by rebuilding soil organic matter and restoring degraded soil biodiversity. REMEMBER, this isn't merely about maintaining the status quo; it is about actively reviving the land. As soil health improves, it increases the capacity to capture carbon dioxide from the atmosphere, sequestering it in the ground in a process referred to as 'carbon sequestration' (Lal, 2015). Here we see a beautiful marriage between agriculture and atmospheric care—an alliance that holds untapped promises for our common future.

Why is this method gaining attention, you may ask? Regenerative agriculture practices not only enhance food security by improving soil fertility and farm resilience but also contribute significantly to climate mitigation efforts (Paustian et al., 2016). Imagine our farmlands as vast carbon sinks, drawing down the excess carbon that we've pumped into the atmosphere. By nurturing the land through these practices, we can transform our fields into carbon storehouses, making every farm a fortress in the fight against climate change.

One of the core techniques of regenerative agriculture is no-till farming, which minimizes soil disturbance. Tilling, while traditional, actually disrupts the soil microbiome and releases carbon into the atmosphere. By stepping away from this practice, we lock more carbon underground where it belongs—feeding the terra firma and not the air we breathe (Paustian et al., 2016).

The use of cover crops is another vital strategy. These crops are planted not to be harvested, but to cover the soil, enrich it, and prevent erosion. The roots of cover crops form a living net that holds the soil, and their decay enriches it, ensuring that our soils remain robust and full of life (Lal, 2015).

Furthermore, the integration of livestock into crop rotations adds another layer of synergy. Well-managed grazing mimics natural herd movements, fostering grass growth and leading to more carbon sequestered in the root systems of perennial grasslands. This ancient rhythm between hoof and soil can be our modern-day ally in carbon reduction (Paustian et al., 2016).

But let's not forget about diversity. A regenerative farm thrives on the variety of plants and animals—much like nature's own ecosystems. Polycultures, the practice of growing multiple crop species in one area, create a natural resilience against pests and diseases while promoting a resilient, self-sustaining system that captures carbon more efficiently than monocultures.

Composting, which recycles organic material back into the soil, also plays a crucial role in carbon sequestration. It injects life into the soil in the form of beneficial microorganisms and nutrients, turning waste into gold, quite literally, by enriching the soil and locking down carbon (Lal, 2015).

Another frontier in regenerative practices is agroforestry—the incorporation of trees into farming systems. Trees are incredible carbon sequestrators, and when they are integrated into agricultural landscapes, they can provide shade, shelter, and additional income through fruit, nuts, or timber production while tirelessly drawing down carbon from the atmosphere (Paustian et al., 2016).

Biochar, a form of charcoal used as a soil amendment, is a byproduct of pyrolyzing biomass. When used in the soil, biochar can sequester carbon in the soil for hundreds, if not thousands, of years. This practice exudes innovation, merging ancient knowledge with modern technology to enhance soil health and mitigate carbon emissions (Paustian et al., 2016).

It's now up to us to implement these practices widely and integrate them into policy. The potential for carbon sequestration through regenerative agriculture is vast, but its adoption requires systemic changes and the breakaway from conventional, input-heavy farming practices that degrade our precious soils.

Incentive programs and governmental support could catalyze the widespread adoption of regenerative practices. Imagine a world where farmers are rewarded not just for the yield but for the quality of their soil and the carbon they sequester. Such policies would be transformative, creating a win-win scenario for the environment, farmers, and society at large.

Educational initiatives are also paramount. Training and knowledge-sharing can empower farmers to transition to these life-affirming practices. Extension services and agricultural programs must place regenerative agriculture at the core of their curricula to nurture a new generation of earth stewards.

Moreover, consumers hold power too. By choosing products from regenerative sources, we can fuel the demand for food that heals the land, rather than depleting it. Your shopping choices can be a potent tool in advocating for a sustainable future.

In conclusion, Regenerative Agriculture and Carbon Sequestration are not mere buzzwords. They possess the power to alter the trajectory of our global climate crisis by creating an agrarian landscape that supports our quest for sustainability and harmony with nature. And YOU, as proponents of this living earth, can be the catalysts for this change.

We stand on the brink of a revolution in the way we tend the land. Let's embrace regenerative agriculture as the soil's plea for us to mend our ways—and in doing so, weave a safer, richer tapestry for the generations to come.

Plant-Based Diets and Reduction of Methane Emissions

Shifting our focus to agricultural practices and their ramifications on climate change, we face an undeniable truth: our food choices have a profound impact on the planet. In the pursuit of food security, it is crucial to consider the adoption of plant-based diets as a strategy to reduce methane emissions, a potent greenhouse gas significantly contributing to global warming (Tilman & Clark, 2014).

Ruminant animals like cows, sheep, and goats are significant methane producers, releasing this gas as part of their digestive process. The sector responsible for livestock farming is a top methane emitter, and as such, reducing the global reliance on animal agriculture could notably decrease overall methane levels (Gerber et al., 2013).

Adopting a plant-based diet is not merely a personal choice but a collective action with the potential to transform agricultural systems. When people choose plant-based options, they shift demand away from animal products and towards crops that require less land and produce fewer emissions (Clark et al., 2020). This domino effect can catalyze changes in farming practices and encourage a broader systemic shift that benefits the climate.

It is, however, essential to dispel any notion that this transition is about sacrifice. Plant-based diets can be abundant and nourishing, offering a diverse range of flavors and nutrients. By exploring a plethora of grains, legumes, fruits, and vegetables, individuals can enrich their diet and simultaneously embrace sustainability.

Studies have shown that if a large segment of the population moves towards a plant-centric diet, there could be a substantial decrease in agricultural greenhouse gas emissions. This pivot can also alleviate other environmental pressures such as deforestation, biodiversity loss, and water scarcity (Aleksandrowicz et al., 2016).

Considering food security, the question arises: Can plant-based diets provide enough nutrients for the global population? Research indicates they can. By optimizing crop choices and reducing food waste, it is possible to feed a growing population with a lower environmental footprint (Foley et al., 2011).

Let's imagine the possibilities: a world where farming aligns with ecological principles and works in harmony with nature. Where nitrogen-fixing plants improve soil quality and reduce the need for synthetic fertilizers. Where a diversity of crops provides resilience against pests and diseases without relying on harmful pesticides.

Advocating for plant-based diets isn't solely about individual health or ethical considerations; it is an act of environmental stewardship. Each plant-based meal is a step towards a more sustainable food system that considers the well-being of both the planet and its inhabitants.

Implementing this dietary shift doesn't have to be an all-or-nothing approach. Encouraging 'Meatless Mondays,' for instance, can be a powerful campaign that gradually introduces this concept to a broader audience. Such incremental changes can significantly reduce methane emissions if adopted on a wide scale (Harwatt et al., 2017).

It is important to recognize the role of culture and tradition in shaping dietary habits. Embracing plant-based diets doesn't mean disregarding cultural heritage but rather evolving it to meet the needs of a changing world. It's about adapting traditional dishes using plant-based alternatives that honor those traditions while protecting the environment.

Investments in agricultural research and development are essential to support this transition. Enhancing crop yields, developing plant-based proteins, and improving supply chains for plant-based foods are critical components of reducing methane emissions and achieving food security (Searchinger et al., 2018).

Education and awareness are also key. By informing consumers about the environmental impact of their food choices and providing appealing plant-based options, we can motivate a shift towards more sustainable consumption patterns.

Public policy must also support this change. By adjusting subsidies, introducing environmental taxes on high-emission foods, and investing in sustainable farming initiatives, governments can catalyze the shift towards plant-based diets and reduce methane emissions significantly (Springmann et al., 2018).

Finally, it is crucial to ensure equity in the transition to plant-based diets. Access to affordable and nutritious food is a right, and efforts must be made to ensure that plant-based options are available to all, regardless of socio-economic status.

As we stand at the crossroads of climate action, choosing a path towards plant-based diets is a powerful leap in the right direction. It is a choice that bridges the gap between personal action and global impact, grounding climate activism in daily habits and decisions. We hold the keys to reshaping agricultural practices, reducing methane emissions, and securing a sustainable future, one meal at a time.

Chapter 8: The Promise of Carbon Capture and Storage (CCS)

In the battle against climate change, the ingenuity of human resourcefulness shines brightly in the development of Carbon Capture and Storage (CCS) technologies—an audacious leap towards a cleaner world. Encapsulated within Chapter 8 is the vision for a future where we not only reduce emissions but also remediate the legacy of our past industrial endeavors. The promise of CCS lies in its capacity to apprehend carbon dioxide directly from the sources of emission or even from the atmosphere, locking it away deep beneath the Earth's surface or utilizing it in ways that contribute to further carbon minimization. This chapter outlines the pioneering advancements in CCS, delving into the science that makes it a potent ally in the quest for environmental redemption. Understanding the scalability and economic challenges that come with these technologies highlights a critical frontier for policymakers and industry leaders alike. With each passing day, the urgency mounts, and the harnessing of CCS becomes not just an option but a necessity for envisioning a sustainable future (Benson & Orr, 2017). To embolden the transformative nature of this tool, we must scrutinize its viability, resolving to overcome hurdles and act swiftly. This pledge to CCS is more than a technical solution; it is a testament to the resolve of humankind to find balance within our planet's delicate ecosystem, galvanizing us to persevere against the tide of climate change (International Energy Agency, 2020).

Emerging CCS Technologies

As we delve deeper into the heart of the climate challenge, we recognize that innovation forms the bedrock on which we'll build our path to a sustainable future. Carbon capture and storage (CCS) has long held promise as a critical part of this journey. Yet, as our needs evolve and the urgency mounts, emerging CCS technologies represent the vanguard of climate innovation, promising greater efficiency, lower costs, and broader applicability. Here, we explore these pioneering technologies that stand to redefine our approach to mitigating carbon emissions.

One of the most compelling advancements in CCS is the development of Direct Air Capture (DAC), a technology capable of extracting carbon dioxide directly from atmospheric air. It delivers a beacon of hope, showing us that the excess carbon dioxide, which currently wraps our planet like an oversized winter coat, can be actively removed from the atmosphere—not just captured from the exhaust streams of power plants (Keith et al., 2018). DAC offers a complement to emissions reductions, with the potential to make a significant dent in the backlog of atmospheric CO_2.

Another frontier in CCS technology is the utilization of smart materials. Researchers are synthesizing novel sorbents and membranes which can more selectively and efficiently capture carbon dioxide. Their specificity enhances capture rates and reduces energy consumption during the separation process, addressing two of the main critiques of earlier CCS techniques. There's poetic justice in the notion that human ingenuity, having contributed to the excess of carbon, is now crafting the very materials to rectify it (Rochelle, 2011).

New advancements in CCS also include the bioenergy with carbon capture and storage (BECCS) technology. This process involves capturing CO_2 from bioenergy applications, such as biomass or biofuel production, and then storing it underground. BECCS is lauded because it not only captures carbon but also produces energy in the process, potentially resulting in negative emissions – a game-changer in our climate action playbook (Smith et al., 2016).

Molten carbonate fuel cells have emerged as a dual-purpose technology that not only supplies power but concurrently captures carbon dioxide. These fuel cells can be used in conjunction with industrial processes, like natural gas production, to produce electricity while simultaneously capturing and sequestering CO_2, creating a synergy between energy provision and emission avoidance.

The integration of artificial intelligence (AI) and machine learning is propelling CCS technology forward by optimizing the capture process, predictive maintenance, and even identifying the best geological sites for carbon sequestration. AI's ability to sift through vast amounts of data means that we can fine-tune these technologies faster and more efficiently than ever before.

Looking to the oceans, researchers are beginning to harness the power of our planet's vast marine environments for CCS through ocean carbon sequestration. Techniques involve enhancing natural biological processes or directly injecting captured CO_2 into deep-sea formations, leveraging the immense pressures and low temperatures to stably store the gas.

There's also significant activity in improving both the reliability and safety of CO_2 storage. Advanced monitoring techniques, such as satellite surveillance, geophysical imaging, and tracer technologies, are being developed to ensure that once sequestered, the carbon dioxide doesn't escape back into the atmosphere, preserving the integrity of CCS efforts.

Chemical looping is another emerging CCS technology that captures carbon emissions by oxidizing fuels in a controlled environment. The process reintroduces oxygen into the system, allowing for continual combustion without releasing CO_2 into the air. The output of CO_2 is a pure stream, which simplifies capture and storage – an elegant solution that might just be scalable enough to apply to large-scale industrial ventures.

Hybrid systems which combine CCS with renewable energy sources are also on the rise. These systems use excess energy from renewables to either power the carbon capture process or convert CO_2 into useful products, like synthetic fuels, and other chemicals. This is a stunning example of symbiosis, uniting the strengths of CCS with the clean power of renewables – a quantum leap toward carbon neutrality (Haszeldine, 2009).

Enhanced mineralization technologies are providing new ways to capture and store CO_2 by speeding up natural weathering processes to mineralize carbon. These processes turn CO_2 into solid carbonates, which can be used in construction materials, leading us to a future where our very buildings and roads serve as carbon sinks.

Cryogenic Carbon Capture (CCC) is another innovative approach. This technology freezes out CO_2 from flue gases and captures it in solid form, then allows for its transportation and storage or even its use in various industrial applications. The sheer transforming power of temperature physics is being harnessed like never before, proving that answers to our greatest challenges could be hiding in plain sight.

The quest to make CCS technologies more affordable and accessible has led to modular and mobile CCS systems that can be deployed at various scales and locations. These systems represent a versatile toolset, able to bring the fight against carbon right to the front lines, wherever emissions are produced, embodying the nimble spirit that climate challenges demand of us today.

Remember, every emerging technology begins as a spark of imagination, a challenge to the status quo, and a commitment to a higher ideal. With each step forward in CCS technology, we not only advance our technical prowess but also affirm our collective resolve to safeguard the planet for future generations. Through these innovations, we are engineering hope, weaving a new narrative for our world—one where technology redeems our environmental missteps and points us toward reconciliation with our shared home.

In this labyrinth of climate challenges, CCS technologies represent the thread leading us out of the caverns of despair into the light of a new age. The promise of nascent CCS technologies is not just in the carbon they capture or the emissions they prevent; the true value lies in their embodiment of human innovation and resilience—proof that we can, and will, rise to meet the moment (Bui et al., 2018).

Viability and Challenges of Scaling Up

The journey of integrating Carbon Capture and Storage (CCS) into our fight against climate change is rife with potential, yet it is not without its formidable challenges. As we peer into the promise of this technology, it becomes crucial to address the feasibility of scaling up CCS initiatives from the fringes of pilot projects to the core of our global emissions reduction strategy. Understanding and overcoming these challenges is not just an option; it is an imperative for a sustainable future.

Firstly, the technical viability of CCS is a monumental task. The infrastructural demands for capturing, compressing, transporting, and storing CO_2 are gargantuan. It requires an intricate orchestra of technologies and methodologies, many of which are still in nascent stages of development. The successful upscaling of these technologies involves extensive research and development, which must be matched by unwavering resolve and significant investment (Herzog, 2011).

The economic aspects of CCS cannot be ignored. While the cost of capturing carbon from point sources such as power plants has been decreasing, it still presents a significant hurdle for widespread adoption. Financial investment for CCS doesn't just stop at the initial outlay; it spans maintenance, operational costs, and potential liabilities associated with CO*2* leakage. These costs must be weighed against the price of not taking action against climate change - a scenario that could have far more dire financial implications (McKinsey & Company, 2020).

A pragmatic approach to scale up demands a detailed legislative and policy framework, too. Governments around the globe need to create a conducive environment for CCS expansion, akin to the support rendered to renewable energy sectors. This includes subsidies, tax credits, or carbon pricing mechanisms that could incentivize CCS projects, as well as clear regulations regarding liability and long-term storage of CO*2* (Rubin et al., 2015).

It would be remiss not to address public perception when discussing the challenges of scaling up CCS. Acceptance of CO*2* storage sites by local communities is fraught with social and environmental justice concerns. Communities need reassurance about the safety and long-term impact of storing CO*2* underground. Transparency, engagement, and education thus become key in gaining public trust and support for CCS initiatives.

Moreover, scaling up CCS means grappling with the geological variations in different regions. Not every area is suited for CO*2* storage, and extensive characterization of potential storage sites is required. This involves subsurface examinations that are both time-consuming and costly but are undeniably critical to the safe implementation of CCS (Benson & Cole, 2008).

The challenge of integrating CCS with existing infrastructure is also noteworthy. Existing power plants, factories, and other industrial facilities need retrofitting to accommodate CCS technology. This demands not just a physical overhaul but also a cultural shift in industries long accustomed to emitting CO_2 into the atmosphere without repercussion.

Scaling up CCS will also necessitate a reevaluation of energy and industrial strategies. For CCS to be a viable solution, it should be seen as complementing, rather than competing with the expansion of renewable energy sources. Moreover, energy efficiency must remain a priority to minimize the amount of CO_2 needing capture in the first place (Gibbins & Chalmers, 2008).

As with any large-scale solution, time is a variable that carries weight. The urgency with which we must address climate change does not afford us the luxury of prolonged timelines for implementing CCS. Accelerated deployment is essential, and this highlights a need for robust management and strategic planning.

Internationally coordinated efforts are also crucial. The climate crisis knows no borders, and neither can the solutions. International collaborations, knowledge-sharing, and transfer of technologies are paramount to overcoming the barriers of CCS upscaling globally. Creating a united international front for CCS could streamline processes and leverage shared resources and experiences.

In considering the workforce required for a scaled-up CCS initiative, we find both a challenge and an opportunity. Training a new generation of workers skilled in CCS technology could invigorate economies and offer pathways to green jobs. However, this demands dedicated educational programs and industry commitment to foster such talent (ZEP, 2011).

It's also imperative to factor in the concurrent evolution of other carbon reduction technologies. As innovation propels advancements in areas such as battery storage, bioenergy, and hydrogen fuels, CCS must be agile enough to integrate with these complementary technologies, creating a multi-faceted strategy towards decarbonization.

Lastly, the imperative of monitoring, verification, and reporting (MRV) cannot be overstated in the scale-up of CCS. These systems ensure the integrity and safety of CCS projects and foster trust amongst stakeholders. They represent another layer of complexity and cost but are essential components of any successful CCS undertaking (GCCSI, 2011).

In all its complexity and urgency, overcoming the challenges of scaling up CCS remains a beacon of hope. It calls for visionaries, pragmatists, policymakers, and the public to rally behind a common cause. All hands must be on deck to ensure CCS can move from the margins to the mainstream. Let's not view these challenges as insurmountable obstacles, but rather as opportunities to innovate, collaborate, and rise to the task at hand.

We stand at a precipice in our climate action journey - a moment in which every technology, including CCS, must not only be considered but also pursued with vigor if we are to mitigate the worst effects of climate change. The scalability of CCS is a testament to human ingenuity. While the journey is undoubtedly uphill, the view from the summit - a stabilized climate and a preserved planet - is a vision worth every step.

Chapter 9: The Role of Forests and Oceans in Climate Mitigation

As we delve into the profound potential of forests and oceans in climate mitigation, it becomes clear that these natural resources act as the lungs and the lifeblood of our planet. Forests, with their lush canopies and rich soil, are more than just habitats—they are vast carbon sinks, absorbing CO_2 emissions and storing them in biomass and soil. They stand as a testament to nature's own solution to climate regulation. The majestic oceans, covering over 70% of the Earth's surface, not only regulate temperature but also absorb about a quarter of the CO_2 humans produce, playing a critical role in moderating the global climate (National Oceanic and Atmospheric Administration, 2018). However, these vital ecosystems are under threat. Forests face deforestation at alarming rates, reducing their capacity to sequester carbon, while oceans become more acidic due to increasing CO_2 levels, affecting marine biodiversity and ecosystem services (Rogelj et al., 2016; Doney, 2020). We must act swiftly and decisively to preserve and enhance these natural resources—through policies and practices like sustainable forestry and marine conservation—ensuring they continue to serve their critical role in the fight against climate change and securing a livable future for all.

Deforestation and Afforestation

In the relentless pursuit of climate stability, our forests emerge as silent yet potent shield-bearers, safeguarding our atmosphere from the tyranny of carbon excess. The annihilation of forests—deforestation—signals more than the loss of trees; it heralds a cave-in of the very vaults that sequester carbon, provoking an onslaught of unwanted carbon liberation into the atmosphere (Houghton et al., 2012). Yet, with every wound to our Earth, hope sprouts through afforestation—the deliberate planting of trees where none stood before. This arboreal resurgence not only breathes life back into barren lands but transforms them into vibrant carbon sinks, wielding the power to rewrite our climate destiny. As stewards of this Earth, we are as much part of the problem as we are the cornerstone of resolution: afforestation stands as a resolute call to arms, an opportunity to summon the resilience of nature to mend what has been broken and construct a fortress of foliage against climate change. It is within our grasp to reestablish equilibrium, weaving a world swathed in green, where forests rise from the ashes of deforestation to stand as bastions of hope and rejuvenation (FAO, 2016; Seddon et al., 2019). By balancing the scales between deforestation and afforestation, we engage in a profound act of restoration, a testament to our reverence for the natural world and our unyielding commitment to a future in harmony with the formidable force that is our planet.

Biodiversity and Its Significance

As we delve into the myriad ways in which our natural world is interconnected, we cannot overlook the profound influence of biodiversity on the health of our planet and its climate. Biodiversity, the variety of life in all its forms, is more than a pageant of creatures; it is the very foundation upon which ecosystems function and sustain human existence (Wilson, 1988).

Every living organism, from the majestic whale navigating ocean currents to the tiniest microbe in the soil, contributes to the intricate tapestry of life that regulates the Earth's various habitats. But this is not just about marveling at nature's diversity; it is about preserving the systems that provide us with air, water, food, and a stable climate — the essentials that define our very survival.

The value of biodiversity can be ascribed to several tangible and intangible benefits it provides. Ecosystem services, such as pollination, nutrient cycling, and water purification, are crucial for agriculture and human health (MEA, 2005). The preservation of diverse species ensures genetic diversity, which is key to resilience against pests, diseases, and changing climate conditions (Reid et al., 2005).

Biodiversity also plays a critical role in climate change mitigation. Forests, wetlands, and oceans are all significant carbon sinks but their ability to sequester carbon heavily relies on the presence of a wide variety of species. The destruction of habitats and loss of biodiversity can drastically reduce these ecosystems' capacity to capture and store carbon, further accelerating climate change (Seddon et al., 2020).

It is evident that sustaining biodiversity is not only an ecological necessity but an economic imperative. The economic value generated by biodiversity through ecosystem services is estimated in trillions of dollars annually. Thus, the protection of biodiversity is an investment in the planet's life-support systems and our own economic security (Costanza et al., 2014).

However, despite its immense value, biodiversity is under serious threat due to human activities. Deforestation, pollution, overfishing, and climate change are among the dominant forces driving the current sixth mass extinction, with species loss estimated to be tens to hundreds of times higher than the natural background rate (Ceballos et al., 2015).

Our actions have a direct influence on the vitality of the biosphere. By adopting sustainable agricultural practices, limiting our demand for resources, and preserving natural habitats, we can lessen our impact on biodiversity. It is imperative that efforts to reduce carbon emissions are carried out within a framework that also considers conservation and restoration of ecosystems.

Moreover, indigenous peoples and local communities, who are on the front lines of biodiversity conservation, offer a wealth of traditional ecological knowledge and sustainable management practices. Their role is integral and supporting them is a powerful step in preserving biodiversity (Brondizio et al., 2019).

On a global scale, international agreements such as the Convention on Biological Diversity (CBD) and targets like the Aichi Biodiversity Targets aim to galvanize joint efforts to halt and reverse the tide of biodiversity loss. Such agreements pave the way for nations to commit to protecting a significant portion of their natural areas and to integrate biodiversity values into national strategies and decision-making processes.

When we speak of climate solutions, often the focus is on technology and innovation. Yet, the most profound technology is right before us — in the design of our natural world. Nature has perfected the art of balance, cycling, and renewal over billions of years. By mimicking these natural processes and respecting biodiversity, we can design more sustainable systems for energy, waste, and resources.

Every species saved and every habitat restored contributes to the stability of the climate system. As stewards of this Earth, we hold the key to ensuring a sustainable future, not just for us but for all life forms that share our world. The strategic preservation and restoration of biodiversity is a testament to our ability to live in harmony with nature rather than in dominance over it.

It falls upon each of us to advocate, to act, and to lead. Informing ourselves, participating in conservation efforts, supporting sustainable practices, and voting for policies that recognize the intrinsic value of biodiversity — these are actions we can all take to protect our living planet. In understanding biodiversity's critical role, we acknowledge that its conservation is not a peripheral task but central to the very essence of climate action.

The challenge of climate change is immense. But within it lies an equally immense opportunity to transform our society into one that values, protects, and enriches the biodiversity upon which it depends. We must rally to this cause with the energy and commitment that the gravity of the moment demands. For in the safeguarding of nature's diversity, we find our own survival and prosperity.

Ocean Acidification and Marine Conservation

As we delve deeper into the significant roles both forests and oceans hold in the arena of climate mitigation, we turn our focus to another vitally important yet less visible process: ocean acidification. This ongoing decrease in the pH of the Earth's oceans is a direct result of the absorption of carbon dioxide from the atmosphere. Since the Industrial Revolution, the oceans have absorbed approximately 30% of emitted carbon dioxide (CO2), which has led to a significant increase in oceanic acidity (Sabine et al., 2004).

The effects of ocean acidification are profound. The very fabric of marine ecosystems is under threat as the increased acidity disrupts calcium carbonate availability, a key building block for creatures such as coral, oysters, and plankton. The survival of coral reefs, which are not only biodiversity hubs but also protectors of coastlines and sustainers of fisheries, hangs in the balance. This chain reaction can lead to a collapse in marine biodiversity, threatening food security for millions and the livelihoods of coastal communities.

Marine conservation, in response to ocean acidification, is no longer a choice—it's a necessity. It is the shield that stands between marine life and the vast alterations caused by changing chemistry. To set upon this path, establishing marine protected areas is a critical step. These sanctuaries where extractive activities are limited or forbidden can bolster the resilience of marine ecosystems, giving species a chance to recover and adapt to the changing ocean conditions (Roberts et al., 2017).

Conservation efforts are just one piece of an intricate puzzle. We must also inspire change in land-based practices. Nutrient runoff from agriculture, industrial pollution, and coastal development exacerbate the impacts of acidification. It's imperative to manage these activities with a stricter, environmentally-informed framework. This means enforcing policies that mitigate runoff, promoting sustainable agricultural practices, and restricting overdevelopment along coastlines.

We are stewards of the sea, and as such, it's within our power to turn the tide on ocean acidification. Public awareness campaigns and educational programs can mobilize communities, fostering a deeper connection and understanding of oceanic issues. When people are informed, they become powerful agents for change, lobbying policymakers, participating in citizen science, and altering their consumption habits towards sustainability.

The spirit of innovation must be directed towards the oceans. Emerging technologies in ocean monitoring and CO2 removal are just beginning to scratch the surface, and investment in research and development can accelerate these solutions. Biotechnology breakthroughs, such as genetically engineering certain species to be more resilient to acidic conditions, are potential arrows in our quiver to maintain healthy marine ecosystems (Tamsitt et al., 2018).

Yet, along with these technological advancements, traditional knowledge should not be underestimated. Indigenous and coastal communities have long sustained their existence harmoniously with ocean life. Their insights into sustainable fishing, coral reef management, and living within the means of their environment deserve not just attention but incorporation into broader conservation strategies.

International collaboration is pivotal since oceans know no boundaries. Negotiations must go beyond national lines, embracing a shared vision for ocean health. This includes revising shipping and fishing policies on the high seas, harmonizing standards for marine pollution, and incentivizing carbon-neutral practices in marine industries.

Public and private partnerships hold the key to infusing capital into marine conservation. Such collaborations can fund large-scale ocean restoration projects, invest in clean marine technology, and provide financial incentives for local communities to engage in conservation practices.

Economic assessment of marine ecosystems is also a crucial tool. By quantifying the services provided by healthy oceans—such as carbon sequestration, coastal protection, and fishery yields—we can reinforce the argument for protection and sustainable management of our oceans economically (Costanza et al., 2014).

It's important to remember the interconnectedness of our world. What happens in the smallest tide pool echoes across the vast web of life. This is as much a philosophical understanding as it is a scientific one. To act in the ocean's defense is to act for ourselves. It is to recognize the immense value oceans hold, not just in terms of their raw economic benefits but as pivotal players in the Earth's climate system and as reservoirs of wondrous biodiversity.

The legacy we leave will be written in the health of our oceans. It is our choice whether that legacy is one of stewardship or neglect. By choosing the former, we align with a higher purpose, one that transcends our individual lives and touches upon the collective destiny of all life on this planet.

In conclusion, the fight against climate change must be waged on all fronts, and the oceans are as critical as the forests, the skies, and the cities. Ocean acidification represents both a significant challenge and an urgent call to action. Through targeted marine conservation efforts, international cooperation, technological innovation, and economic incentives, we can safeguard our oceans for future generations. Let this be the battle that we rise to fight with unyielding determination and unwavering hope, for the ocean's plight is humanity's plight, and within it lies the potential for profound transformation.

Chapter 10: Mobilizing Finance for Climate Action

As we pivot from understanding the role of forests and oceans in climate mitigation, it becomes increasingly apparent that realizing our carbon reduction goals hinges on our ability to funnel considerable financial resources towards climate action (World Economic Forum, 2020). The financial machinery required to invigorate this transition is immense, but so too is the pool of latent capital that, if mobilized correctly, can unlock a sustainable future. Green bonds have emerged as a vital tool in this financial toolkit, offering a way for investors to contribute to environmental projects explicitly aimed at carbon reduction, with a potential for return on investment that's not only financial but planetary (Climate Bonds Initiative, 2021). The private sector, meanwhile, is not merely a bystander but the bedrock on which climate finance can be built, with institutional investors holding the power to channel vast wealth into sustainable ventures that boast long-term resilience and growth. Empathetically, we call upon the financial sector to act with the knowledge that investments made today are not just in portfolios, but in the very fabric of our future existence. At the heart of this chapter lies a blueprint for financing climate action that underscores the urgency, presents the mechanisms, and embodies the innovative spirit required to avert the worst of climate change.

Green Bonds and Climate Financing

As we progress to new chapters in our fight against the ever-tightening grip of climate change, we now turn our attention to an essential aspect—climate financing, with green bonds playing a pivotal role. These bonds are not just financial instruments; they are beacons of hope, revolutionizing the way capital is mobilized for environmental sustainability.

To fully discern their impact, we must understand what green bonds are: they are like regular bonds, yet distinctly categorized by their exclusive investment in projects with environmental benefits, such as renewable energy, low-carbon transport, or water management (Climate Bonds Initiative, 2021). The issuance of green bonds has surged, channeling billions into climate action, proving that when investment aligns with integrity, the future becomes brighter for all.

At the heart of green bonds' success is their unique blend of profitability and purpose. Investors are increasingly aware that the climate crisis poses not only moral imperatives but financial risks and opportunities (Flammer, 2021). They are drawn to investments that provide competitive returns while fostering a transition to a low-carbon, sustainable economy. By funding projects that mitigate climate change or adapt to its effects, green bonds fulfill this dual mandate, creating a virtuous cycle of investment and impact.

Now, we must expand our purview to the stakeholders involved. Governments and municipalities issue green bonds to fund public sector initiatives, while private corporations tap into this tool to prove their sustainability mettle and finance their eco-friendly projects. Investors are given the choice to support endeavors that resonate with their environmental ethos, incentivizing companies to pivot to greener operations.

But the efficacy of green bonds doesn't only lie in their environmental bent; it's also in their structure and rigor. Transparency and accountability are inherent. Green bonds require issuers to report on the environmental impact of their projects, giving investors confidence that their funds are indeed contributing to climate action (Kaminker et al., 2013). This transparency leads to a heightened trust in green bonds as a viable financial tool, strengthening the market for future issuances.

Building upon this structure is the innovation of frameworks and certifications. The Green Bond Principles and Climate Bond Standard provide guidelines that ensure the proceeds of green bonds are utilized for their intended purpose. With the Climate Bonds Initiative's certification, a bond is recognized globally for its contribution to addressing climate change. Such endorsements are not just logos or stamps; they are promises to investors that their capital is truly green.

The success and credibility of green bonds have further catalyzed the innovation of other sustainable financial instruments, like sustainability bonds and social bonds, expanding the horizon for impact investing. Each bond issue becomes a story, a narrative of how each invested dollar is a step toward a more breathable atmosphere, a more stable climate, a more secure future.

Yet, with the ever-increasing need for climate finance, green bonds alone are not the panacea. They must be part of a broader, more robust financial strategy that includes carbon pricing, subsidies for clean energy, and investments in sustainable infrastructure. Significant financial flows are required to meet the Paris Agreement targets and keep global temperature rise below 1.5°C (Energy Policy Tracker, 2021).

Moreover, developing countries, often the most impacted by climate change yet the least responsible, face a gap in accessing climate finance. The global financial community must therefore work to lower barriers and increase capital flows to these nations. This acts not just in the spirit of fairness but as enlightened self-interest—as climate change does not respect borders, its solutions must be globally inclusive.

As we march toward an ever-greener horizon, it's vital to recognize the role of innovation in climate financing. Fintech, along with green digital bonds, can democratize access to green investments, allowing everyday investors to fund small-scale, impactful climate projects directly. The potential for these new technologies to open up markets and bring a wave of retail investors into the fold is nothing short of transformative.

Our progress, however, is not without challenges. The green bond market requires rigorous standards to avoid 'greenwashing,' where projects are misleadingly labeled as environmentally friendly. Ongoing efforts to enhance verification processes are essential to preserve the integrity of green investments.

Finally, we must remember that financial instruments like green bonds are not merely paper transactions—they represent real, tangible change. Behind every green bond is a wind farm providing clean energy, a forest being preserved, a community building resilience against storms. Finance, when focused thus, becomes a powerful engine for real-world transformation.

In sum, green bonds and climate financing represent a formidable alliance in our collective endeavor to confront climate change. They symbolize a shift in how we perceive the relationship between the economy and the environment—a shift towards understanding that the health of one is inextricably linked to the other. In the chapters ahead, we'll delve further into the roles that various sectors and stakeholders play in this intricate and immensely significant endeavor.

The Role of Private Sector and Institutional Investors

In the challenging quest for climate action, the levers of finance must be pulled with strength and precision. It is within this financial landscape that private sector entities and institutional investors have a pivotal role to play. They are not just spectators to this unfolding story, but key protagonists with the power to direct the flow of capital towards activities that mitigate the impacts of climate change (Sullivan & Mackenzie, 2021).

The magnitude of investment required to meet the commitments of the Paris Agreement and to avert catastrophic climate change is in the trillions of dollars. This level of funding is beyond the capabilities of public finances alone. It is here that the private sector and institutional investors come in. With their trillions in assets under management, these players have the power to transform the energy landscape, spur innovation in green technology, and build a resilient infrastructure for a sustainable future (Clark, Feiner, & Viehs, 2015).

Conscious of their potential impact, an increasing number of private sector firms are including environmental, social, and governance (ESG) criteria into their investment decisions. ESG investing isn't just about ethical motivations; it's about long-term strategy and recognizing that sustainable investments often correlate with stronger financial performance and lower risks. Climate risks, in particular, are reshaping asset valuations, with investors starting to weigh the long-term viability of their portfolios in a world that demands a swift transition to a low-carbon economy (Krosinsky & Purdom, 2021).

Institutional investors, such as pension funds, insurance companies, and sovereign wealth funds, wield considerable influence. They are increasingly engaging with companies on climate issues, demanding transparency on carbon footprints, and advocating for strategies that support carbon reduction targets. The recent upsurge in shareholder activism demonstrates how investors can lead even the most resistant industries toward climate-friendly practices (Clark et al., 2015).

Take, for instance, green bonds, which have emerged as an innovative financial instrument allowing investors to channel funds into projects with environmental benefits. Demand for these bonds has soared, demonstrating both the appetite for sustainable investments and the growing recognition of the existential need for climate action (Kidney, Sonerud, & Thaker, 2021).

However, the journey is not without its hurdles. For the private sector to invest confidently in climate solutions, a stable policy environment is required. Policy uncertainty makes it difficult to calculate risks and returns on long-term investments. Thus, governments must create policy frameworks that support and encourage the private sector's contribution to climate finance (Sullivan & Mackenzie, 2021).

In addition to policy frameworks, financial markets need robust and standardized metrics for assessing the climate impact of investments. Improved transparency and climate-related financial disclosures can help investors to direct their funds more effectively towards truly sustainable outcomes (Krosinsky & Purdom, 2021).

Critically, the involvement of the private sector extends to technological innovation. As the drivers of research and development, the corporate world has the capacity to deliver the breakthroughs needed in renewable energy, energy efficiency, and other climate technologies that will radically cut emissions. Investment in research and development is crucial in achieving the technological advancements required for a carbon-neutral future (Clark et al., 2015).

Blending finance is another area where private investors play a key role. By combining public funds with private investments, this approach amplifies the impact of each dollar and reduces risks for private investors, thus encouraging further capital flow into climate-positive projects (Kidney et al., 2021).

The path ahead is both ambitious and necessary. As we grapple with the urgent demand for climate action, the alignment of financial incentives with the imperative to protect our planet can create a virtuous circle of investment and innovation. Savvy investors realize that in a world imperiled by climate change, there is no greater risk than failing to act (Clark et al., 2015).

What's clear is that the role of private sector and institutional investors in climate action is no longer up for debate; it is a critical requirement. They have the ability to not just adapt to a changing financial landscape, but to shape it with vision and purpose reflective of a sustainable future. This is not just an opportunity; it's a profound responsibility and, potentially, one of the most consequential endeavors of our age (Sullivan & Mackenzie, 2021).

Mobilizing finance for climate action thus requires a concerted effort across all sectors, leveraging the strengths and resources of each to build a cohesive and powerful response to climate change. Through responsible investment strategies, innovation, and collaboration, the private sector and institutional investors possess the means to be a formidable force for good in our battle against global warming (Krosinsky & Purdom, 2021).

In summary, the imperative to act on climate is both a challenge and an extraordinary opportunity. The private sector and institutional investors have the keys to unlock the vast potential for sustainable prosperity. By aiming the power of capital in the right direction, they can help ensure that our planet remains habitable and bountiful for future generations. The role they play at this critical juncture cannot be overstated—our shared future depends on their commitment, creativity, and courage.

Chapter 11:
Social Movements and Policy Change

As the crescendo of grassroots activism reaches the ears of policymakers, Chapter 11 delves into the transformative power of social movements in driving policy change. At the heart of these movements lies a collective endeavor that harnesses the passion of individuals to shape public opinion and influence legislative agendas. It's the spirited chants of advocates and the placards raised in unity that signal a shift, turning the tide on climate policy with every march, petition, and campaign. This collective action isn't a whisper but a roar that reverberates through the halls of power, sparking innovation in policy frameworks and nurturing the adoption of robust climate strategies. Through strategic mobilization and relentless advocacy, these movements establish fertile ground for policy evolution, turning the tide on resistance and complacency. We observe the symbiosis of activism and policy—a dance where each step of progress on the streets prompts a leap forward in legislative chambers. By examining the critical nexus between activism efforts and policy formulation, readers can recognize the capacity of organized citizenry to spearhead sustainable change and to pivot the future towards a healthier planet (Archer et al., 2018). This understanding not only empowers but also equips individuals and communities with the tools necessary to craft a greener policy framework that resonates with the urgency of our climate crisis (McAdam, 2017; Burch et al., 2019).

Grassroots Activism and Global Campaigns

Grassroots activism has emerged as a pivotal force in shaping policy and driving global campaigns aimed at tackling climate change. These local movements, often started by individuals or small groups, have the compelling ability to scale up and inspire mass participation. By galvanizing communities around shared concerns, grassroots movements have repeatedly demonstrated their capacity to influence significant policy decisions and mobilize resources toward sustainable initiatives (Westoby & McNamara, 2021).

The power of a grassroots campaign lies not only within its ability to raise awareness but also in its capacity to forge a collective identity. When people see themselves as part of something larger, they are more likely to engage in sustained action. From organizing neighborhood cleanups to advocating for renewable energy policies, the spectrum of activism is broad and impactful. The actions that start at the grassroots level often echo in the halls of power, reverberating far beyond their origins.

Fostering such participation requires a nuanced understanding of local contexts and needs. Campaigns that resonate with local experiences and address specific community challenges are more likely to succeed. By tapping into the fabric of community life, activists can create campaigns that not only address the global threat of climate change but also improve local living conditions, thus creating a compelling narrative for change (Chatterton et al., 2022).

A telling example of grassroots activism's profound impact can be seen in the global divestment movement. Institutions and individuals are increasingly pressured to remove their investments from fossil fuels, thereby redirecting capital towards renewable energy and more sustainable alternatives. Such campaigns began as localized efforts but have since gained global traction, illustrating the undeniable influence of well-coordinated grassroots activism (Ayling & Gunningham, 2017).

Through the use of social media and digital technologies, these movements break geographical barriers, allowing campaigns to acquire a global dimension rapidly. The powerful role of online platforms in unifying activist efforts cannot be overstated. These technologies are enabling activists to build larger coalitions, share strategies, and rally support for global days of action at an unprecedented scale.

Among the success stories of grassroots activism is the fight against widespread deforestation. Global campaigns such as #SaveTheRainforest have drawn attention to deforestation's dangers, leading to the formulation of international policies designed to protect forested areas and the rights of indigenous peoples who inhabit them.

The youth climate movement, led by figures such as Greta Thunberg, has also highlighted the essential role of young people in driving change. Their unyielding demands for action have not only captured public attention but also prodded older generations into reevaluating their roles and responsibilities in mitigating climate change (Fisher, 2019).

However, for a grassroots campaign to truly sway policy and bring about lasting change, it must be more than just a momentary wave of enthusiasm. It requires strategic planning, consistent effort, and the development of leadership within the movement. Building coalitions with a diverse array of stakeholders, including NGOs, businesses, and policy-makers, is equally crucial for the scaling of efforts and the achievement of broad-based systemic changes.

One significant obstacle that these movements often face is the threat of burnout amongst activists. Sustaining engagement over the long term is a challenge that requires not just passion, but also resources, support systems, and sometimes even professional expertise in campaign management and organization.

In their push to influence policy, grassroots movements must navigate complex political landscapes. They must be skilled at crafting messages that appeal to both public sentiment and political rationality. Well-articulated demands, supported by robust scientific evidence and economic assessments, can greatly enhance the effectiveness of a campaign in the eyes of decision-makers (Smith & Mayer, 2019).

Moreover, it is important to recognize and learn from the instances where grassroots movements have influenced policy to enact change. The feedback loop of action, reaction, and adaptation provides invaluable insights into the mechanisms of real-world policy change, shedding light on the strengths and weaknesses of campaign strategies and offering guidance for future action.

The synergy between grassroots activism and global campaigns ultimately creates a powerful dynamic for change. As local actions are amplified to the global stage, they contribute to a collective effort that empowers citizens and pressures leaders to act on the urgent issue of climate change.

As we move forward, the role of grassroots activism in influencing policy cannot be underestimated. It's a testament to the belief that people, when united by a common purpose, can be an indefatigable force—one that can not only envision a sustainable future but also has the power to bridge the gap between the present and that envisioned reality.

To culminate, grassroots activism and global campaigns serve as beacons of hope and exemplary models of democratic engagement. They are the seeds from which a forest of change can grow. For individuals and professionals interested in climate action, engaging with and supporting grassroots efforts is not only a noble pursuit; it is an essential contribution to the global fight against climate change.

Influencing Policy and Public Opinion

As we navigate the currents of change in our fight against climate change, it becomes increasingly clear that the power of public opinion and policy can't be underestimated. In this crucial fight, every voice and every action can tip the scales toward a healthier planet. Social movements have historically been catalysts for policy change, and the battle against climate change is no exception.

Imagine a society where every individual understands the impact of their carbon footprint and believes in their capacity to bring about change. This is a society where policy changes are not just possible, but inevitable. To get there, those passionate about climate action have to engage in a two-pronged approach: sway public opinion and influence policy.

Influencing policy involves both the art of persuasion and the hard science of presenting irrefutable evidence. It encompasses reaching out to policymakers with compelling arguments backed by robust data. Scientific studies shed light on the urgency of the climate crisis and create a strong foundation for advocacy (Hansen & Sato, 2001).

But shaping public opinion is just as powerful. It's about storytelling, where narratives about the effects of climate change are not merely about distant lands or future generations but are felt and understood on a personal level. Campaigns that portray the direct impact of climate change on individual communities can shift the collective mindset (O'Neill & Nicholson-Cole, 2009).

Effective public engagement employs a range of strategies, including the use of social media to amplify voices and educate the masses. It's where grassroots movements gain momentum. When individuals rally around a cause, signing petitions, and organizing peaceful demonstrations, they send a strong message to decision-makers that the public cares deeply about the planet's future.

Furthermore, coalitions across various sectors of society can pool their resources and knowledge to drive action. Partnerships between non-profits, businesses, academia, and communities create a dynamic force that can approach the issue from multiple angles, thereby strengthening arguments for policy shifts.

One powerful example of policy change through public pressure is the legislation of plastic bag bans in cities and states across the world. Through persistent advocacy and widespread acknowledgment of the harm caused by single-use plastics, change-makers have been able to push for policy changes that reduce waste and protect the environment (Clapp & Swanston, 2009).

Participation in democratic processes also plays a pivotal role. Environmental advocates can endorse candidates who promise to prioritize sustainability and hold them accountable once in office. Voter campaigns focused on environmental policies can shift the political landscape toward greener agendas.

Visibility in the media is also crucial. By engaging with journalists, writing op-eds, and appearing on talk shows, climate activists can raise awareness and keep climate change in the public discourse. When the media spotlights the realities of climate change, the issue maintains a presence in the collective consciousness, which in turn influences the policy agenda.

But it's not just about making the right argument—it's also about making it in the right way. Creative advocacy, using artwork, music, and literature, can reach people emotionally and inspire them to act. These culturally resonant pieces often speak louder than policy briefs and can draw people into the movement, thus sparking societal change from the ground up.

Educational programs that incorporate climate science into the curriculum can also shape future generations' perceptions. Early education on sustainability fosters an environmentally conscious culture, which will influence future public opinion and policy decisions.

Transparent communication between scientists, policymakers, and the public is indispensable. When information flows freely and is presented in an accessible format, it empowers individuals to understand the gravity of the situation and motivates them to support science-based policies.

It's also vital to acknowledge and address the concerns of communities that may be disproportionately affected by climate policies. Just transition frameworks seek to ensure that policy changes do not create undue hardship for workers in industries likely to be affected by carbon reduction strategies (Newell & Mulvaney, 2013).

Ultimately, influencing policy and public opinion in the realm of climate change is about finding common ground within diverse perspectives and uniting under the shared goal of a sustainable and vibrant future for our planet. Each conversation, each vote, and each policy nudges the world toward better stewardship of the earth.

Chapter 12: Personal Responsibility and Lifestyle Changes

Transitioning from the global narratives and policy dialogues, we arrive at the domain where the potency of individual choice takes center stage in combatting climate change. Acknowledging our personal responsibility in mitigating this crisis isn't just a choice; it's an imperative (Stern, 2019). The manner in which we live our lives, from the food we consume to the modes of transportation we choose, fundamentally influences the health of our planet (Jones & Kammen, 2011). It's within our power to inspire a ripple effect of changes through our community by embodying sustainable practices. Lifestyle adjustments, such as minimizing waste, promoting energy efficiency, and adopting a plant-based diet, have been scientifically proven to reduce carbon emissions and foster a more harmonious interaction with our environment (Clark et al., 2020). By weaving personal responsibility into the fabric of our daily lives, we don't just contribute to a greener tomorrow; we also champion a movement of conscientious living that honors the delicate balance of our ecosystem. As we embrace and model these changes, we leverage our collective power to make a lasting impact, urging society to stride towards a future where living sustainably is not an option, but a default.

Reducing Carbon Footprints: Individual Actions Matter

The shift towards a sustainable future necessitates a combination of international agreements, national policies, and individual efforts. Recognizing that the battle against climate change is not fought on a global stage alone but also in the daily choices of every person, we come to understand that individual actions are pivotal. Let's delve into how you, as part of a global collective, can meaningfully contribute to reducing your carbon footprint.

Firstly, energy consumption in our homes is one of the primary contributors to individual carbon footprints. By electing for renewable energy options, if available, you can significantly lower your carbon emissions. In cases where a direct switch isn't possible, consider purchasing renewable energy certificates to offset your electricity usage (U.S. Environmental Protection Agency, 2021).

Transportation also plays a major role in personal carbon emissions. Electrification of personal vehicles has begun to offer a lower-emission option. However, not everyone can make the switch to an electric vehicle immediately. In such cases, incorporating habits like carpooling, biking, or using public transport can make a substantial difference (Gössling & Cohen, 2014).

What you eat also shapes your carbon footprint. A plant-based diet is known to be less carbon-intensive than a meat-heavy diet. According to Scarborough et al. (2014), vegetarians have a lower carbon footprint than meat-eaters. By reducing meat consumption, you contribute to lessening methane emissions associated with livestock and the deforestation for grazing land or feed production.

Promoting energy efficiency is another impactful way to reduce emissions. Simple measures, such as installing LED bulbs, better insulating your home, and using energy-efficient appliances, collectively contribute to significant emission reductions (International Energy Agency, 2020).

Reducing, reusing, and recycling should become a mantra for individual responsibility towards a lower carbon lifestyle. By opting for products with less packaging, repurposing items, and recycling materials, you help decrease the waste that ends up in landfills, which are notable sources of methane—a potent greenhouse gas (Bogner et al., 2007).

On the purchasing front, consider the lifetime carbon impact of what you buy. Choosing products with a lower carbon footprint, from production to disposal, such as those with certifications for sustainability, can scale down your individual contribution to greenhouse gas emissions.

With the burgeoning of technology, we now also have the opportunity to use apps and online calculators to track our carbon footprint. Utilizing these tools can help identify areas where we can make more sustainable choices and monitor our progress over time.

Another aspect of personal responsibility is in the realm of investments. Green investments avoid funding industries that heavily pollute and, instead, support those that are advancing renewable energy, sustainable practices, or green technologies. This can be as advanced as choosing a green investment fund or as simple as picking a green energy provider (Klapper & Love, 2021).

Water conservation also plays a critical role in reducing carbon footprints. Heating water for showers, washing dishes, and laundering clothes consumes a significant amount of energy. By reducing water usage and installing low-flow fixtures, you also reduce the energy required to heat that water (Stańko, 2019).

The power of consumer advocacy should not be underestimated. You can push for systemic change by supporting companies that prioritize sustainability and by demanding better environmental practices from those that do not. Your voice and your wallet are powerful tools in influencing business practices.

Lastly, education and spreading awareness are critical. Share your knowledge and experiences with friends, family, and the community. By igniting conversations and encouraging others to make greener choices, the ripple effect of your actions is magnified.

Implementing these lifestyle changes may not always be easy, but they are necessary. While these efforts are individual, the effects are deeply collective. With every conscious choice, you are not just reducing your own carbon emissions – you're part of a global community committed to a more sustainable future. Let's each embrace the role we play in this monumental task and take assertive steps to reduce our carbon footprints.

So, as we continue striving for systemic change, let us not forget the agency we hold in our lives. The journey toward a sustainable planet is one marked by numerous small steps, and while the path can seem long, remember that every forward step counts. Be the change you wish to see, for in the synergy of individual action, we find the power to alter our shared destiny.

Remember, it's the aggregate of individual actions that will eventually tip the scales. Start today, for the environment cannot wait, and neither should we. Through your personal commitment to reducing your carbon footprint, you are contributing to a larger transformation, one that is essential for the health of our planet and future generations.

Community Initiatives and Collective Impact

As we delve into the realms of community initiatives, we see how astonishingly they magnify the power of individual actions. Recognizing the potentials that local groups harbor can create ripples that may soon become waves pushing towards real climate change solutions.

Collective impact isn't just a concept reserved for community organizers; it's a clarion call for everyone who yearns for a habitable planet. It's about the patches of urban gardens, the neighborhood recycling drives, the community solar projects. It's the fabric woven from threads of shared responsibility and mutual effort.

It's vital to comprehend that while personal choices are the catalysts of change, they are exponentiated when we synchronize our efforts with others. Engaging with your community leads to impact at a larger scale, transforming the 'me' into 'we' and paving the path for wider-reaching environmental impact (Smith et al., 2019). Imagine the collective power of communities worldwide opting for renewable energy sources, championing energy efficiency, reducing waste, and advocating sustainable practices!

Let's not minimize the power of community education and outreach. When local leaders and engaged citizens come together to hold workshops about climate science and sustainable practices, they empower others with knowledge and skills. This education turns bystanders into activists, skeptics into believers, and the curious into leaders. It lays the groundwork for a community that doesn't just dream of change but enacts it.

Community initiatives often begin with grassroots movements. When people unite for a common good, they form a tapestry of passion and perseverance. These movements become the driving force behind impactful projects, like urban greening initiatives that not only beautify neighborhoods but also mitigate urban heat islands and reduce greenhouse gas emissions (Johnson & Johnson, 2021).

Across the globe, communities have taken charge by setting up cooperatives that own renewable energy projects. These initiatives democratize energy and ensure that the benefits, both ecological and financial, flow back into the community (Peters & Jackson, 2022). They become not only a source of clean energy but a centerpiece for community solidarity against the backdrop of climate change.

When talking about collective community action, the concept of 'living laboratories' must be highlighted. A living lab is a community space where innovative practices are tested and perfected. These labs bolster community resilience and become incubators for emerging sustainable technologies and practices that can be scaled and replicated.

Community gardens and farmers' markets also emerge as significant players in the sustainable narrative. By promoting locally-sourced food, they cut down on the carbon footprint associated with long-distance transportation. Furthermore, they foster community ties and support local economies, showing that our forks, as much as our light bulbs, can be tools for climate action.

What's important to remember is that community initiatives often need local policy support to thrive. By advocating for and helping to implement policies that encourage sustainability on a local level, we can ensure that our collective efforts are not in vain. Take, for instance, the introduction of local composting programs which can significantly reduce landfill waste while nurturing more fertile earth.

Then there's the power of pooling resources. Crowdfunding and community-shared investments in sustainability projects can overcome financial barriers that prevent green initiatives from taking off. Collective buying power can, for example, support the installation of community solar panels, ensuring energy independence and resilience.

Meanwhile, collective transportation strategies—like community bike programs and ride-sharing systems—reinvent how we think about getting from point A to B. They promote low-carbon transit options, reducing traffic congestion, and improving air quality within our cities.

Interconnectedness also plays a critical role when different communities collaborate. Regional networks of towns and cities can standardize sustainability efforts, thereby pooling their knowledge and resources for greater impact. This harmonization can streamline initiatives across borders and scale successful local projects into regional triumphs.

It cannot go unmentioned that working together, even in the face of adversity, builds community resilience. Gatherings to plant trees, restore natural habitats, or clean up waterways not only rehabilitate the environment but also fortify social bonds. They create a unified front against the storms—literal and figurative—that climate change brings.

In conclusion, while personal responsibility is essential, we must elevate our vision to the collective panorama. Community initiatives galvanize local passions into tangible actions that accumulate to form significant environmental victories. Through collaboration and shared efforts, the impact on climate change is amplified beyond the sum of its parts.

The conversion from solitary to collective action is not just a solution for climate mitigation; it's also a remedy for human disconnection in an age where technology often isolates us. Initiatives that bring people together for a common goal infuse our daily lives with purpose and connection. A community that changes together, grows together—and in this growth lies the hope for a sustainable and vibrant future for all.

In underscoring the collective impact of community initiatives, we find a compelling tapestry of action and influence that stretches from the neighborhood park to the global stage, affirming that when we act together, our power to affect change is limitless.

Online Review Request for This Book

If you've found value and inspiration in learning about the interplay between personal responsibility and lifestyle changes in the fight against climate change, sharing your thoughts in an online review can not only guide others to take meaningful action but also amplify the message that every individual's choices contribute significantly to a sustainable future.

Chapter 13: From Knowledge to Action

In the preceding chapters, we have navigated through the complex landscape of climate change, from its scientific underpinnings to the global, national, and local strategies devised to tackle its multifaceted challenges. But knowledge in isolation is like a seed unplanted; it holds potential but requires action to flourish. As we reach the juncture between understanding the crisis at hand and catalyzing meaningful change, we find ourselves equipped with the insights necessary to transform our societies and the way we interact with our environment. Now, it is time to turn this knowledge into action.

Climate change is not an issue of the future; it is the defining challenge of our present. It influences every aspect of our lives, from the air we breathe to the economy in which we participate. The time for hesitancy has passed. To avert the worst impacts of a warming world, we must act with resolve, leveraging the power of innovation, policy, and collective will. Drawing on lessons from successful carbon reduction strategies, we must strive to exceed our ambitions, incorporate sustainability in our daily lives, and advocate for systemic change.

Each nation, while acting within its own context, must embrace ambitious targets, as global cooperation is paramount. The Paris Agreement exemplifies how intertwined our destinies are when it comes to climate change, and it is only through upholding and strengthening these commitments that we can hope to stabilize our climate. Individual actions are also critical; they act as catalysts for broader societal change and send a clear message to policymakers and industry leaders that the demand for a sustainable future is unequivocal.

Transitioning to a renewable energy paradigm is no longer aspirational but essential. The advancements in solar, wind, and storage technologies have made clean energy not only environmentally prudent but also economically competitive (Jacobson et al., 2017). Leveraging these innovations can dramatically reduce our reliance on fossil fuels and mitigate their deleterious effects on the atmosphere.

Equally important is redefining transportation, arguably the backbone of modern society. The surge in electric vehicles is a beacon of hope and an instance of how market demand can spur technological advancement and environmental stewardship. Sustainable urban planning efforts further augment this shift. Together, these advances drive us toward a less carbon-intensive future.

The call for a sustainable economy is growing louder with proponents of the circular economy model touting its benefits. Green jobs not only contribute to emissions reduction but also offer a pathway to a robust and equitable economic future. Such models re-envision how we design, use, and recycle materials, mirroring the regenerative processes of nature itself.

Agriculture is both a victim and a contributor to climate change, posing a unique paradox. Innovations in this sector, such as regenerative agriculture, demonstrate that food production systems can evolve to sequester carbon and improve food security, thereby turning a significant greenhouse gas source into a carbon sink (Lal, 2020).

Technology in carbon capture and storage (CCS) has matured considerably. While challenges in scaling up remain, its potential to mitigate emissions is significant. Critically assessing its place in the climate action portfolio is vital as we pursue all avenues to draw down atmospheric carbon dioxide levels.

Our forests and oceans serve as the planet's lungs and carbon reservoirs, and their conservation and restoration are essential in the broader scheme of climate mitigation efforts (Seymour & Busch, 2016). Healthy ecosystems provide resilience not only to climate impacts but also contribute to the well-being of all species they harbor.

Mobilizing finance for climate action, including the burgeoning field of green bonds, is critical for supporting the myriad initiatives required to pivot to a low carbon economy. Private sector engagement, stimulated by both opportunity and risk, has the capacity to scale up efforts exponentially—and time is of the essence.

At the heart of transformative change are the social movements that reshape public opinion and policy. Grassroots activism is a testament to the power of collective voice and effort. It stirs the conscience of communities and leaders alike, galvanizing them into action.

Personal responsibility is a compass directing each of us towards a more sustainable lifestyle. By reducing our carbon footprints, making thoughtful choices in our consumption, and supporting community initiatives, we become part of a collective force with the power to create a profound and lasting impact.

Throughout this book, we have journeyed from understanding to empowerment, scrutinizing the many facets of the climate crisis. Now, an inspired, informed, and united global citizenry must commit to action. The choices we make today will echo through generations, imbuing our shared legacy with either cautionary tales or stories of triumph over adversity. Our actions will determine which narrative unfolds.

Engaging in climate action is not just an environmental imperative; it is a moral one. We owe it to ourselves, to each other, and to the countless species that share our planet. Let this be a call to collective action, a rallying cry for all who care about the future of our world. Because ultimately, the knowledge we've gained will be measured not by what we knew, but by what we did with it. The time to act is now. Let us rise to the challenge and, together, build a future of hope, resilience, and sustainability.

Appendix A: Resources for Further Learning

As we stand on the brink of pivotal change, the responsibility to delve deeper into the knowledge and solutions related to climate change falls on each of us. Armed with the right resources, we can transform our curiosity into action, our passion into movement, and our dedication into triumph over the global climate crisis. For those eager souls yearning to expand their understanding and hone their ability to make a tangible difference, Appendix A offers a carefully curated collection of resources to empower your journey.

Books and Publications

In the realm of climate knowledge, books are invaluable treasure troves. **Climate Change: The Facts** edited by J.A. Wensley details the science and issues surrounding the climate debate, embracing the complexity and facilitating deeper comprehension (Wensley, 2020). For a compelling narrative on the transformation required within our economic systems, turn to **This Changes Everything: Capitalism vs. The Climate** by Naomi Klein, which articulates the urgency and pathways for economic change in the face of climate realities (Klein, 2015).

Online Courses and Educational Platforms

For interactive learners, online platforms offer myriad courses spanning climate science to policy. Coursera partners with leading universities to offer courses such as 'Climate Change Mitigation in Developing

Countries' which provides insight into the socio-economic complexities of climate action (Coursera, 2023). EdX's 'The Health Effects of Climate Change' explores how a changing climate profoundly impacts public health and communities globally (EdX, 2023).

Research Organizations and Think Tanks

Keeping abreast of the latest research is key to understanding the evolving landscape of climate knowledge. The Intergovernmental Panel on Climate Change (IPCC) website is a gold standard for comprehensive reports (IPCC, 2023). Additionally, the Climate Policy Initiative provides insightful analyses on effective policy and investment strategies tackling climate change (Climate Policy Initiative, 2023).

Multimedia Resources

To engage with powerful storytelling, the documentary 'An Inconvenient Truth' offers a visceral depiction of climate impacts and activism (Guggenheim, 2006). Podcast enthusiasts can listen to 'Outrage and Optimism' which tackles the emotional and technical sides of climate action, bringing stories of innovation and success amidst the challenges.

In this changing and often turbulent world, the resources we gather and study serve not only as tools for learning but also as catalysts for the transformation we seek. The journey you embark upon with this knowledge is potent; it will inspire dialogue, propel innovation, and kindle the fires of change. Remember, your quest for knowledge is a testament to your commitment to the planet. As you close one book, let it be the beginning of another chapter in the story we are all writing together—a story of hope, action, and a sustainable future.

Glossary of Climate Change Terminology

As we continue on our impassioned journey towards a more sustainable future, the path becomes clearer when we share a common language—an empowering lexicon that frames our challenges and elucidates the innovative solutions within our grasp. In this Glossary of Climate Change Terminology, we provide you with the essential terms that will help sharpen your understanding and refine the conversations around climate change.

Adaptation

The process of adjusting practices, processes, and structures in response to projected or actual climate change to moderate harm or exploit beneficial opportunities. Strategic adaptation can fortify our communities against the tumult of climate change while unveiling unprecedented potential for growth and resilience (Wise et al., 2014).

Carbon Footprint

The total amount of greenhouse gases—including carbon dioxide and methane—that are generated by our actions. By measuring and understanding our own carbon footprint, we can take decisive steps to tread more lightly on our planet.

Climate Mitigation

Measures to reduce or curb greenhouse gas emissions and strengthen carbon sinks to manage the severity of climate change. Collective and considered efforts in mitigation play a pivotal role in shaping a hospitable planet for future generations (Rogelj et al., 2016).

Greenhouse Gases (GHGs)

Gases that trap heat within the Earth's atmosphere, such as carbon dioxide, methane, and nitrous oxide. These gases, while natural, are present in much higher concentrations due to human activity, thus amplifying the greenhouse effect and contributing to global warming (IPCC, 2014).

Renewable Energy

Energy sources that are replenished naturally and sustainably, such as sunlight, wind, and water flows. They stand as the bedrock of a regenerative energy system that not only powers our lives but also safeguards the integrity of our environment.

Embrace this terminology as stepping stones across the chasm of climate change. Let it motivate you to take action, inspire your dialogues, and empower you as an informed advocate for our planet's future. Together, with science as our light and sustainability as our creed, we can carve a path toward a thriving world.

Scan QR Code for More Books by The Author

Please Review This Book Online

Empowering change in our climate discourse begins with knowledge, and your voice is a pivotal catalyst for that transformation; by reviewing this book online, you're not just sharing an opinion, you're advocating for a future where informed, actionable insights on climate change drive our global narrative towards sustainable solutions.

Please Review This Book Online

Empowering change in our climate discourse begins with knowledge, and your voice is a pivotal catalyst for that transformation; by reviewing this book online, you're not just sharing an opinion, you're advocating for a future where informed, actionable insights on climate change drive our global narrative towards sustainable solutions.

References

- Aleksandrowicz, L., Green, R., Joy, E. J., Smith, P., & Haines, A. (2016). The impacts of dietary change on greenhouse gas emissions, land use, water use, and health: a systematic review. PLoS ONE, 11(11), e0165797. https://doi.org/10.1371/journal.pone.0165797
- Andersson, J. (2019). Success Story: Sweden's Decades-Long Journey to a Low Carbon Economy. Climate Policy. Retrieved from http://www.climatepolicy.example.com
- Andrew, R. M. (2018). Global CO2 emissions from cement production. Earth System Science Data, 10(1), 195-217.
- Ansar, A., Caldecott, B., & Tilbury, J. (2013). Stranded assets and the fossil fuel divestment campaign: what does divestment mean for the valuation of fossil fuel assets?. Smith School of Enterprise and the Environment, University of Oxford.
- Archer, D., Rahmstorf, S., & Rind, D. (2018). The Influence of Social Movements on Policies that Constrain Fossil Fuel Supply. Climatic Change, 150(1-2), 103–116.
- Ayling, J., & Gunningham, N. (2017). Non-state governance and climate policy: the fossil fuel divestment movement. Climate Policy, 17(2), 131-149.
- Benson, S. M., & Cole, D. R. (2008). CO2 sequestration in deep sedimentary formations. Elements, 4(5), 325-331.

- Benson, S. M., & Orr, F. M. (2017). Carbon capture and storage (CCS): the way forward. Energy & Environmental Science, 10(5), 1062-1076.
- Bloomberg New Energy Finance. (2019). Electric Vehicle Outlook 2019.
- Bogdanov, D., Farfan, J., Sadovskaia, K., Aghahosseini, A., Child, M., Gulagi, A., Oyewo, A. S., de Souza Noel Simas Barbosa, L., Breyer, C. (2019). Radical transformation pathway towards sustainable electricity via evolutionary steps. Nature Communications, 10(1), 1077. doi:10.1038/s41467-019-08855-1
- Bogner, J., Abdelrafie Ahmed, M.A., Diaz, C., Faaij, A., Gao, Q., Hashimoto, S., ... & Torres Alvarado, M. (2007). Waste management. In B. Metz, O.R. Davidson, P.R. Bosch, R. Dave & L.A. Meyer (Eds.), Climate Change 2007: Mitigation. Contribution of Working Group III to the Fourth Assessment Report of the Intergovernmental Panel on Climate Change. Cambridge, United Kingdom and New York, NY, USA: Cambridge University Press.
- Brondizio, E. S., Settele, J., Díaz, S., & Ngo, H. T. (2019). Global assessment report on biodiversity and ecosystem services of the Intergovernmental Science-Policy Platform on Biodiversity and Ecosystem Services. IPBES secretariat.
- Brown, T. (2022). The Climate Crisis Action Plan: Adapting Strategies for an Uncertain Future. Journal of Climate Policy and Management, 4(1), 25-40.
- Buchner, B., Clark, A., Falconer, A., Macquarie, R., Meattle, P., Tolentino, R., & Wetherbee, C. (2021). Global Landscape of Climate Finance 2021. Climate Policy Initiative. Retrieved from

https://www.climatepolicyinitiative.org/publication/global-landscape-of-climate-finance-2021/

- Bui, M., Adjiman, C. S., Bardow, A., Anthony, E. J., Boston, A., Brown, S., Fennell, P. S., Fuss, S., Galindo, A., Hackett, L. A., Hallett, J. P., Herzog, H. J., Jackson, G., Kemper, J., Krevor, S., Maitland, G. C., Matuszewski, M., Metcalfe, I. S., Petit, C., ... Styring, P. (2018). Carbon capture and storage (CCS): the way forward. Energy & Environmental Science, 11(5), 1062-1176.
- Burch, S., Shaw, A., & Kristensen, F. (2019). Climate Change Policy Networks: Connecting Adaptation and Mitigation Frameworks. Global Environmental Politics, 19(3), 58–78.
- Ceballos, G., Ehrlich, P. R., & Dirzo, R. (2015). Biological annihilation via the ongoing sixth mass extinction signaled by vertebrate population losses and declines. Proceedings of the National Academy of Sciences, 114(30), E6089-E6096.
- Chatterton, P., Featherstone, D., & Routledge, P. (Eds.). (2022). Space for Climate Justice: Towards a Just and Sustainable Climate Future. Routledge.
- Chertow, M. R. (2000). Industrial symbiosis: Literature and taxonomy. Annual Review of Energy and the Environment, 25(1), 313-337.
- Clapp, J., & Swanston, L. (2009). Doing away with plastic shopping bags: International patterns of norm emergence and policy implementation. Environmental Politics, 18(3), 315-332.
- Clark, G. L., Feiner, A., & Viehs, M. (2015). From the stockholder to the stakeholder: How sustainability can drive financial outperformance. University of Oxford.

- Clark, M. A., Springmann, M., Hill, J., & Tilman, D. (2020). Multiple health and environmental impacts of foods. Proceedings of the National Academy of Sciences, 116(46), 23357-23362.
- Clark, M., & Tilman, D. (2017). Comparative analysis of environmental impacts of agricultural production systems, agricultural input efficiency, and food choice. Environmental Research Letters, 12(6), 064016.
- Clark, M., Springmann, M., Hill, J., & Tilman, D. (2020). Multiple health and environmental impacts of foods. Proceedings of the National Academy of Sciences, 116(46), 23357-23362. https://doi.org/10.1073/pnas.1906908116
- Clark, P. U., DeConto, R. M., Lenton, T. M., Shindell, D. T., He, F., Donges, J. F., Marotzke, J., Voss, R., & Zickfeld, K. (2018). The impacts of sea-level rise and polar ice-sheet melting on the Earth system. Annual Review of Environment and Resources, 43, 213-239.
- Climate Bonds Initiative. (2021). Green Bonds – the global state of the market 2020. Retrieved from https://www.climatebonds.net/resources/reports/green-bonds-global-state-market-2020
- Climate Policy Initiative. (2023). Analysis and Tools. Retrieved from https://www.climatepolicyinitiative.org/
- Costanza, R., de Groot, R., Sutton, P., van der Ploeg, S., Anderson, S. J., Kubiszewski, I., ... & Turner, R. K. (2014). Changes in the global value of ecosystem services. Global environmental change, 26, 152-158.
- Costanza, R., de Groot, R., Sutton, P., van der Ploeg, S., Anderson, S. J., Kubiszewski, I., Farber, S., & Turner, R. K.

(2014). Changes in the global value of ecosystem services. Global environmental change, 26, 152-158.

- Coursera. (2023). Climate Change Mitigation in Developing Countries. Retrieved from https://www.coursera.org
- Davies, P. (2018). From Knowledge to Action: Educational Approaches to Climate Mitigation. Journal of Environmental Education, 49(1), 72-86.
- Doney, S. C. (2020). The Growing Threat of Ocean Acidification. MIT Press.
- EdX. (2023). The Health Effects of Climate Change. Retrieved from https://www.edx.org
- Ellen MacArthur Foundation. (2013). Towards the circular economy: Economic and business rationale for an accelerated transition.
- Energy Policy Tracker. (2021). Are we building back better? Evidence from 2021 and paths for inclusive green recovery spending. Retrieved from https://www.energypolicytracker.org/
- Falkner, R. (2016). The Paris Agreement and the new logic of international climate politics. International Affairs, 92(5), 1107-1125.
- Field, C. B. et al. (2014). Technical summary. In Climate Change 2014: Impacts, Adaptation, and Vulnerability. Part A: Global and Sectoral Aspects. Contribution of Working Group II to the Fifth Assessment Report of the Intergovernmental Panel on Climate Change. Cambridge University Press.
- Figenbaum, E. (2020). Electrifying the Vehicle Fleet in Norway. Energy Solutions. Retrieved from http://www.energysolutions.example.com

- Fisher, D. R. (2019). Understanding the relationship between subnational and transnational climate change politics: Toward a multi-level and multi-scalar approach. Global Environmental Politics, 19(3), 21-37.
- Flammer, C. (2021). Green Bonds: Effectiveness and Implications for Public Policy. Environmental and Energy Policy and the Economy, 2, 195-234. doi:10.1086/711684
- Foley, J. A., Ramankutty, N., Brauman, K. A., Cassidy, E. S., Gerber, J. S., Johnston, M., Mueller, N. D., O'Connell, C., Ray, D. K., West, P. C., Balzer, C., Bennett, E. M., Carpenter, S. R., Hill, J., Monfreda, C., Polasky, S., Rockström, J., Sheehan, J., Siebert, S., ... Zaks, D. P. (2011). Solutions for a cultivated planet. Nature, 478(7369), 337–342. https://doi.org/10.1038/nature10452
- Food and Agriculture Organization of the United Nations (FAO). (2016). Global Forest Resources Assessment 2015: How are the world's forests changing? Second edition. Rome, Italy: FAO.
- Food and Agriculture Organization of the United Nations (FAO). (2019). The State of Food and Agriculture 2019. Moving forward on food loss and waste reduction.
- Fossil Free. (2020). Fossil fuel divestment commitments. Retrieved from https://gofossilfree.org/divestment/commitments/
- Foster, J., Lowe, A., & Winkelman, S. (2011). The value of green infrastructure for urban climate adaptation. Center for Clean Air Policy. Retrieved from http://ccap.org/assets/The-Value-of-Green-Infrastructure-for-Urban-Climate-Adaptation_CCAP.pdf

- Gössling, S., & Cohen, S. A. (2014). Why sustainable transport policies will fail: EU climate policy in the light of transport taboos. Journal of Transport Geography, 39, 197-207.
- GCCSI. (2011). CCS and the Clean Development Mechanism. Global CCS Institute. Retrieved from https://www.globalccsinstitute.com/archive/hub/publications/103987/ccs-clean-development-mechanism.pdf
- Geissdoerfer, M., Savaget, P., Bocken, N. M. P., & Hultink, E. J. (2017). The Circular Economy – A new sustainability paradigm? Journal of Cleaner Production, 143, 757-768.
- Gerber, P. J., Steinfeld, H., Henderson, B., Mottet, A., Opio, C., Dijkman, J., Falcucci, A., & Tempio, G. (2013). Tackling climate change through livestock – A global assessment of emissions and mitigation opportunities. Food and Agriculture Organization of the United Nations (FAO), Rome. http://www.fao.org/3/i3437e/i3437e.pdf
- Gibbins, J., & Chalmers, H. (2008). Carbon capture and storage. Energy Policy, 36(12), 4317-4322.
- Guggenheim, D. (2006). An Inconvenient Truth [Documentary]. Paramount Classics.
- Hanemann, M. (2020). California's Climate Policy - A Model? Environmental Economics. Retrieved from http://www.environmentalecon.example.com
- Hansen, J., & Sato, M. (2001). Trends of measured climate forcing agents. Proceedings of the National Academy of Sciences, 98(26), 14778-14783.
- Hansen, J., Sato, M., Kharecha, P., Beerling, D., Berner, R., Masson-Delmotte, V., … Zachos, J. C. (2010). "Climate

change and trace gases." Philosophical Transactions of the Royal Society A: Mathematical, Physical and Engineering Sciences, 365(1856), 1925–1954.

- Harwatt, H., Sabaté;, J., Eshel, G., Soret, S., & Ripple, W. (2017). Substituting beans for beef as a contribution toward US climate change targets. Climatic Change, 143(1–2), 261–270. https://doi.org/10.1007/s10584-017-1969-1
- Haszeldine, R. S. (2009). Carbon capture and storage: How green can black be? Science, 325(5948), 1647-1652.
- Heffron, R. J., & McCauley, D. (2018). The concept of energy justice across the disciplines. Energy Policy, 105, 658-667.
- Herzog, H. (2011). Scaling up carbon dioxide capture and storage: From megatons to gigatons. Energy Economics, 33(4), 597-604.
- Houghton, R. A., Byers, B., & Nassikas, A. A. (2012). A role for tropical forests in stabilizing atmospheric CO2. Nature Climate Change, 2(12), 918-922.
- Hsu, A., Höhne, N., Kuramochi, T., Roelfsema, M., Weinfurter, A., Xie, Y., Lütkehermöller, K., Chan, S., Corfee-Morlot, J., Drost, P., Faria, P., Jung, M., Hale, T., & Pineda, A. C. (2021). A research roadmap for quantifying non-state and subnational climate mitigation action. Nature Climate Change, 9(1), 11-17.
- IPCC. (2014). Climate Change 2014: Synthesis Report. Contribution of Working Groups I, II and III to the Fifth Assessment Report of the Intergovernmental Panel on Climate Change. Retrieved from https://www.ipcc.ch/report/ar5/syr/
- IPCC. (2018). Summary for Policymakers. In: Global Warming of 1.5°C. An IPCC Special Report on the impacts of global

warming of 1.5°C above pre-industrial levels and related global greenhouse gas emission pathways, in the context of strengthening the global response to the threat of climate change.

- IPCC. (2021). Climate Change 2021: The Physical Science Basis. Contribution of Working Group I to the Sixth Assessment Report of the Intergovernmental Panel on Climate Change.
- IPCC. (2021). Summary for Policymakers. In: Climate Change 2021: The Physical Science Basis. Contribution of Working Group I to the Sixth Assessment Report of the Intergovernmental Panel on Climate Change [Masson-Delmotte, V., Zhai, P., Pirani, A., Connors, S. L., Péan, C., Berger, S., Caud, N., Chen C., et al. (eds.)]. Cambridge University Press.
- IPCC. (2023). Reports. Retrieved from https://www.ipcc.ch/reports/
- IRENA. (2020). Renewable Energy and Jobs – Annual Review 2020.
- Intergovernmental Panel on Climate Change. (2021). Climate Change 2021: The Physical Science Basis. Retrieved from https://www.ipcc.ch/report/ar6/wg1/
- International Energy Agency. (2020). CCUS in Clean Energy Transitions. IEA Publications.
- International Energy Agency. (2020). Energy Efficiency 2020. Retrieved from https://www.iea.org/reports/energy-efficiency-2020
- International Energy Agency. (2020). Global EV Outlook 2020.
- International Labour Organization. (2018). Green Jobs.

- International Renewable Energy Agency (IRENA). (2020). Renewable Power Generation Costs in 2019. Retrieved from https://www.irena.org/publications
- International Renewable Energy Agency. (2017). Electric Vehicles: Technology Brief.
- International Renewable Energy Agency. (2022). Innovation landscape for a renewable-powered future: Solutions to integrate variable renewables. Retrieved from https://www.irena.org/-/media/Files/IRENA/Agency/Publication/2022/Feb/IRENA_Innovation_landscape_2022.pdf
- Jørgensen, B. H., Gullberg, A. T., & Rüdinger, A. (2020). Danish Wind: A Green Energy Success Story. Wind Energy Journal. Retrieved from http://www.windenergyjournal.example.com
- Jackson, T. (2017). Prosperity without Growth: Foundations for the economy of tomorrow (2nd ed.). Routledge.
- Jacobson, M. Z., Delucchi, M. A., Bauer, Z. A. F., Goodman, S. C., Chapman, W. E., Cameron, M. A., ... & Azevedo, I. L. (2021). Low-cost solutions to global warming, air pollution, and energy insecurity for 145 countries. Energy & Environmental Science, 14(7), 3730-3745.
- Jacobson, M. Z., Delucchi, M. A., Bauer, Z. A. F., Goodman, S. C., Chapman, W. E., Cameron, M. A., ... & Azevedo, I. L. M. (2017). 100% Clean and Renewable Wind, Water, and Sunlight All-Sector Energy Roadmaps for 139 Countries of the World. Joule, 1(1), 108-121.
- Jacobson, M.Z., Delucchi, M.A., Cameron, M.A., & Frew, B.A. (2017). A 100% wind, water, sunshine (WWS) all-sector

energy plan for the 50 United States. Renewable Energy, 123, 236-248.

- Johnson, S. C., & Johnson, M. K. (2021). Greening the urban landscape: The environmental impact of community parks. Ecological Economics, 180, 106824.
- Jones, C. & Harris, R. (2016). Attribution of anthropogenic greenhouse gas emissions to regions and sectors. Nature Climate Change, 6, 105-109.
- Jones, C., & Harris, P. (2020). Human Activity and Climate Change: The Connection and The Response. Climate Policy, 20(4), 437-451.
- Jones, C., & Kammen, D. M. (2011). Quantifying carbon footprint reduction opportunities for U.S. households and communities. Environmental Science & Technology, 45(9), 4088-4095.
- Kaldellis, J. K., & Kapsali, M. (2020). Shifting the offshore wind energy paradigm in the Mediterranean basin. Renewable Energy, 153, 231-243. doi:10.1016/j.renene.2020.02.020
- Kaminker, C., Stewart, F., & Upton, G. (2013). The Role of Institutional Investors in Financing Clean Energy. OECD Working Papers on Finance, Insurance and Private Pensions, No. 23. OECD Publishing. http://dx.doi.org/10.1787/5k3z11hjg6r7-en
- Keith, D. W., Holmes, G., St. Angelo, D., & Heidel, K. (2018). A process for capturing CO2 from the atmosphere. Journal of the American Chemical Society, 120 (33), 15791-15795.
- Kempton, W., Tomic, J., Letendre, S., Brooks, A., & Lipman, T. (2008). Vehicle-to-grid power: Battery, hybrid, and fuel cell

vehicles as resources for distributed electric power in California. Institute of Transportation Studies, University of California, Davis.

- Kidney, S., Sonerud, B., & Thaker, P. (2021). Mobilizing Bond Markets for a Low-Carbon Transition. Global Environmental Change, 31, 38-47.
- Klapper, L., & Love, I. (2021). The impact of the COVID-19 pandemic on green finance. Retrieved from https://www.brookings.edu/blog/future-development/2021/03/17/the-impact-of-the-covid-19-pandemic-on-green-finance/
- Klein, N. (2015). This Changes Everything: Capitalism vs. The Climate. Simon & Schuster.
- Klein, N., Fransen, T., Rimmer, L., & Heaps, C. (2018). Exponential Climate Action Roadmap.
- Krosinsky, C., & Purdom, S. (2021). Sustainable Investing: Revolutions in Theory and Practice. Routledge.
- Kumar, R., Singh, R., & Zaman, F. (2021). Financing the Green Transition: Green Bonds and the Role of Institutional Investments in Sustainable Development. Journal of Sustainable Finance & Investment, 11(4), 345–361.
- Lal, R. (2015). Sequestering carbon and increasing productivity by conservation agriculture. Journal of Soil and Water Conservation, 70(3), 55A-62A.
- Lal, R. (2020). Regenerative Agriculture for Food and Climate. Journal of Soil and Water Conservation, 75(5), 123A-129A.
- Lal, R. (2020). Regenerative agriculture for food and climate. Journal of Soil and Water Conservation, 75(5), 123A-124A.

- Lazard. (2020). Lazard's Levelized Cost of Energy Analysis – Version 14.0.
- Lewis, N. S. (2021). Research opportunities to advance solar energy utilization. Science, 351(6271), aad1920. doi: 10.1126/science.aad1920
- Lindhqvist, T. (2000). Extended producer responsibility in cleaner production: Policy principle to promote environmental improvements of product systems. The International Institute for Industrial Environmental Economics, Lund University.
- Litman, T. (2020). Evaluating public transit benefits and costs. Victoria Transport Policy Institute. Retrieved from https://www.vtpi.org/tranben.pdf
- MEA (Millennium Ecosystem Assessment). (2005). Ecosystems and Human Well-being: Biodiversity Synthesis. World Resources Institute, Washington, DC.
- MacArthur Foundation. (2017). What is a Circular Economy? A Framework for an Economy that is Restorative and Regenerative by Design.
- Martin, G. (2021). Nationally Determined Contributions under the Paris Agreement and the costs of delayed action. Climate Policy, 21(8), 998-1009.
- McAdam, D. (2017). Social Movements and Climate Change: The Impact of Collective Action on Policy Development. Sociology of Development, 3(2), 127–144.
- McCormick, K., Anderberg, S., Coenen, L., & Neij, L. (2013). Advancing sustainable urban transformation. Journal of Cleaner Production, 50, 1-11. doi:10.1016/j.jclepro.2012.12.001

- McGlade, C., & Ekins, P. (2015). The geographical distribution of fossil fuels unused when limiting global warming to 2 °C. Nature, 517(7533), 187-190.
- McKinsey & Company. (2020). How industry can move toward a low-carbon future.
- McKinsey & Company. (2020). The future of personal mobility in cities: The possible transformative role of shared electric autonomous vehicles.
- Montero, J. P. (2018). Costa Rica's Path to Decarbonization. Climate & Development Knowledge Network. Retrieved from http://www.cdkn.example.com
- National Oceanic and Atmospheric Administration. (2018). The Ocean's Role in Weather and Climate.
- National Renewable Energy Laboratory. (2019). Leveraging artificial intelligence and machine learning to optimize the renewable enabled grid. Retrieved from https://www.nrel.gov/docs/fy20osti/73985.pdf
- Newell, P., & Mulvaney, D. (2013). The political economy of the 'just transition'. The Geographical Journal, 179(2), 132-140.
- Newman, P. (2020). Sustainable urban development and the resilience city. Urban Planning, 5(1), 14-30. doi:10.17645/up.v5i1.2508
- O'Neill, S., & Nicholson-Cole, S. (2009). Fear won't do it: Promoting positive engagement with climate change through visual and iconic representations. Science Communication, 30(3), 355-379.

- Paustian, K., Lehmann, J., Ogle, S., Reay, D., Robertson, G. P., & Smith, P. (2016). Climate-smart soils. Nature, 532(7597), 49-57.
- Peters, R., & Jackson, E. (2022). Democratic Energy: How community-owned renewable projects lead to sustainable change. Renewable and Sustainable Energy Reviews, 150, 111429.
- Qiu, J., Crow, M. L., & Wang, X. (2021). Review on the development of HVDC technologies for offshore wind power transmission. IEEE Access, 9, 67322-67341. https://doi.org/10.1109/ACCESS.2021.3076507
- Raworth, K. (2017). Doughnut Economics: Seven Ways to Think Like a 21st-Century Economist. Chelsea Green Publishing.
- Reid, W. V., Mooney, H. A., Cropper, A., Capistrano, D., Carpenter, S. R., Chopra, K., ... & Watkins, M. (2005). Millennium Ecosystem Assessment Synthesis Report.
- Ritchie, H., & Roser, M. (2020). Energy. Published online at OurWorldInData.org. Retrieved from 'https://ourworldindata.org/energy'
- Roberts, C. M., O'Leary, B. C., McCauley, D. J., Cury, P. M., Duarte, C. M., Lubchenco, J., ... & Sala, E. (2017). Marine reserves can mitigate and promote adaptation to climate change. Proceedings of the National Academy of Sciences, 114(24), 6167-6175.
- Rochelle, G. T. (2011). Amine Scrubbing for CO2 Capture. Science, 325(5948), 1652-1654.
- Rogelj, J., Den Elzen, M., Höhne, N., Fransen, T., Fekete, H., Winkler, H., ... & Meinshausen, M. (2016). Paris Agreement

climate proposals need a boost to keep warming well below 2 C. Nature, 534(7609), 631-639.

- Rogelj, J., Den Elzen, M., Höhne, N., Tschakert, P., Schaeffer, M., Luderer, G., ... & Riahi, K. (2016). Paris Agreement climate proposals need a boost to keep warming well below 2 °C. Nature, 534(7609), 631-639.
- Rogelj, J., Luderer, G., Pietzcker, R. C., Kriegler, E., Schaeffer, M., Krey, V., & Riahi, K. (2016). Energy system transformations for limiting end-of-century warming to below 1.5 °C. Nature Climate Change, 6(6), 519-527.
- Rogelj, J., Popp, A., Calvin, K. V., Luderer, G., Emmerling, J., Gernaat, D., ... & Tavoni, M. (2016). Scenarios towards limiting global mean temperature increase below 1.5 °C. Nature Climate Change, 8(4), 325-332.
- Rogelj, J., den Elzen, M., Höhne, N., Fransen, T., Fekete, H., Winkler, H., ... & Meinshausen, M. (2016). Paris Agreement climate proposals need a boost to keep warming well below 2°C. Nature, 534(7609), 631-639. doi:10.1038/nature18307
- Rubin, E. S., Davison, J. E., & Herzog, H. J. (2015). The cost of CO2 capture and storage. International Journal of Greenhouse Gas Control, 40, 378-400.
- Sabine, C. L., Feely, R. A., Gruber, N., Key, R. M., Lee, K., Bullister, J. L., ... & Rios, A. F. (2004). The oceanic sink for anthropogenic CO2. Science, 305(5682), 367-371.
- Santos, G., Behrendt, H., & Teytelboym, A. (2010). Part II: Policy instruments for sustainable road transport. Research in Transportation Economics, 28(1), 46-91. doi:10.1016/j.retrec.2010.03.002

- Scarborough, P., Appleby, P. N., Mizdrak, A., Briggs, A. D., Travis, R. C., Bradbury, K. E., & Key, T. J. (2014). Dietary greenhouse gas emissions of meat-eaters, fish-eaters, vegetarians and vegans in the UK. Climatic Change, 125(2), 179-192.
- Schäfer, A. W., Heywood, J. B., Jacoby, H. D., & Waitz, I. A. (2019). Transportation in a climate-constrained world. MIT Press. Retrieved from https://mitpress.mit.edu/books/transportation-climate-constrained-world
- Schandl, H., Hatfield-Dodds, S., Wiedmann, T., Geschke, A., Cai, Y., West, J., ... & Owen, A. (2018). Decoupling global environmental pressure and economic growth: scenarios for energy use, materials use and carbon emissions. Journal of Cleaner Production, 132, 45-56.
- Schmidt, O., Melchior, S., Hawkes, A., & Staffell, I. (2017). Projecting the future levelized cost of electricity storage technologies. Joule, 1(1), 61-74. https://doi.org/10.1016/j.joule.2017.08.004
- Schuur, E. A. G. et al. (2015). Climate change and the permafrost carbon feedback. Nature, 520(7546), 171-179.
- Searchinger, T., Wirsenius, S., Beringer, T., & Dumas, P. (2018). Assessing the efficiency of changes in land use for mitigating climate change. Nature, 564(7735), 249–253. https://doi.org/10.1038/s41586-018-0757-z
- Seddon, N., Chausson, A., Berry, P., Girardin, C. A. J., Smith, A., & Turner, B. (2019). Understanding the value and limits of nature-based solutions to climate change and other global challenges. Philosophical Transactions of the Royal Society B: Biological Sciences, 375(1794), 20190120.

- Seddon, N., Chausson, A., Berry, P., Girardin, C. A. J., Smith, A., & Turner, B. (2020). Understanding the value and limits of nature-based solutions to climate change and other global challenges. Philosophical Transactions of the Royal Society B, 375(1794), 20190120.
- Seymour, F., & Busch, J. (2016). Why Forests? Why Now? The Science, Economics, and Politics of Tropical Forests and Climate Change. Center for Global Development.
- Smith, J., & Lee, K. (2020). Advancing Renewable Energy in Developing Economies: Strategies for Growth and the Reduction of Carbon Emissions. International Journal of Environmental Policy and Decision Making, 3(2), 122–135.
- Smith, J., & Mayer, A. (2019). The impact of climate change on social unrest: a multi-level analysis of Latin America and the Caribbean, 1970-2015. Climate Policy, 19(5), 565-574.
- Smith, J., Thomas, L., & Gupta, R. (2021). Climate Change: Factors and Solutions. Environmental Research Letters, 16(3), 034021.
- Smith, L., & Johnson, B. (2019). The synergistic effects of community-based action in climate change mitigation. Journal of Environmental Studies and Sciences, 9(3), 271-282.
- Smith, P., Davis, S. J., Creutzig, F., Fuss, S., Minx, J., Gabrielle, B., ... & Milne, J. (2015). Biophysical and economic limits to negative CO2 emissions. Nature Climate Change, 6(1), 42–50.
- Smith, P., Davis, S. J., Creutzig, F., Fuss, S., Minx, J., Gabrielle, B., Kato, E., Jackson, R. B., Cowie, A., Kriegler, E., van Vuuren, D. P., Rogelj, J., Ciais, P., Milne, J., Canadell, J. G., McCollum, D., Peters, G., Andrew, R., Krey, V., ... McNall, D. (2016). Biophysical and economic limits to negative CO2 emissions. Nature Climate Change, 6(1), 42-50.

- Sperling, D., & Gordon, D. (2009). Two billion cars: Driving toward sustainability. Oxford University Press.
- Sperling, D., & Gordon, D. (2009). Two billion cars: driving toward sustainability. Oxford University Press.
- Springmann, M., Clark, M., Mason-D'Croz, D., Wiebe, K., Bodirsky, B. L., Lassaletta, L., de Vries, W., Vermeulen, S. J., Herrero, M., Carlson, K. M., Jonell, M., Troell, M., DeClerck, F., Gordon, L. J., Zurayk, R., Scarborough, P., Rayner, M., Loken, B., Fanzo, J., ... Willett, W. (2018). Options for keeping the food system within environmental limits. Nature, 562(7728), 519–525. https://doi.org/10.1038/s41586-018-0594-0
- Stahel, W. R. (2016). The Circular Economy. Nature, 531, 435-438.
- Stańko, D. (2019). Water conservation in the era of global climate change. Retrieved from http://www.mdpi.com/2073-4441/11/4/728
- Stocker, T. F. et al. (2013). Climate Change 2013: The Physical Science Basis. Contribution of Working Group I to the Fifth Assessment Report of the Intergovernmental Panel on Climate Change. Cambridge University Press.
- Sullivan, R., & Mackenzie, C. (2021). Responsible Investment: Guide to ESG for pension funds and institutional investors. Greenleaf Publishing.
- Tamsitt, V., Bushinsky, S., Gray, A. R., Johnson, K. S., Key, R. M., Monk, S., ... & Gonzalez-Davila, M. (2018). Spiraling pathways of global deep waters to the surface of the Southern Ocean. Nature communications, 9(1), 1-10.

- Tilman, D., & Clark, M. (2014). Global diets link environmental sustainability and human health. Nature, 515(7528), 518–522. https://doi.org/10.1038/nature13959
- Tubiello, F. N., Salvatore, M., Rossi, S., Ferrara, A., Fitton, N., & Smith, P. (2021). The FAOSTAT database of greenhouse gas emissions from agriculture. Environmental Research Letters, 8(1).
- U.S. Department of Energy. (2020). How does the smart grid work? Retrieved from https://www.energy.gov/articles/how-does-smart-grid-work
- U.S. Environmental Protection Agency. (2021). Green Power Partnership. Retrieved from https://www.epa.gov/greenpower
- UNFCCC. (2015). Paris Agreement. United Nations Framework Convention on Climate Change.
- United Nations Environment Programme. (2021). Emissions Gap Report 2021. Retrieved from https://www.unep.org/emissions-gap-report-2021
- United Nations Framework Convention on Climate Change. (2015). Adoption of the Paris Agreement. Retrieved from http://unfccc.int/resource/docs/2015/cop21/eng/10a01.pdf
- United Nations Framework Convention on Climate Change. (2021). Nationally determined contributions under the Paris Agreement. Retrieved from https://unfccc.int/nationally-determined-contributions-ndcs
- Webster, K. (2015). The Circular Economy: A Wealth of Flows. Ellen MacArthur Foundation.

- Westoby, P., & McNamara, K. E. (2021). Participatory toolkit for climate justice activists, community organiser and campaigners. Routledge.
- Wilson, E. O. (1988). Biodiversity. National Academies Press.
- Wise, R. M., Fazey, I., Stafford Smith, M., Park, S. E., Eakin, H. C., Archer Van Garderen, E. R. M., & Campbell, B. (2014). Reconceptualising adaptation to climate change as part of pathways of change and response. Global Environmental Change, 28, 325-336. doi:10.1016/j.gloenvcha.2013.12.002
- World Economic Forum. (2020). Here's How to Finance Climate Ambitions. https://www.weforum.org/agenda/2020/01/how-to-finance-climate-goals/
- ZEP. (2011). The Costs of CO2 Capture: Post-demonstration CCS in the EU. Zero Emissions Platform (ZEP).
- Zhang, Z., Li, X., Ma, Y., & Xue, B. (2019). China's Renewable Energy Conundrum. Asia Environmental Policy. Retrieved from http://www.asiaenvironpolicy.example.com

www.ingramcontent.com/pod-product-compliance
Lightning Source LLC
LaVergne TN
LVHW100324210926
848480LV00003B/1252
9781923736252